The

Southern Way

The regular volume for the Southern devotee

Kevin Robertson

Issue 56

ISBN 9781800350274

First published in 2021 by Noodle Books
an imprint of Crécy Publishing Ltd

New contact details
All editorial submissions to:
The Southern Way (Kevin Robertson)
'Silmaril'
Upper Lambourn
Hungerford
Berkshire RG17 8QR
Tel: 01488 674143
editorial@thesouthernway.co.uk

A CIP record for this book is available from the British Library

Publisher's note: Every effort has been made to identify and correctly attribute photographic credits. Any error that may have occurred is entirely unintentional.

Printed in the UK by Short Run Press

Noodle Books is an imprint of
Crécy Publishing Limited
1a Ringway Trading Estate
Shadowmoss Road
Manchester M22 5LH

www.crecy.co.uk

Front cover:
Platform 1 at Southampton Central plays host to USA No. 30073 in the process of running light to Eastleigh depot probably from the Western Docks. (The other possibility would be from Redbridge sleeper works.) At the time, 1965, the up main platform had yet to be 'modernised' which saw the removal of the clock tower and its replacement by a concrete office block to be known as 'Overline House'. Look carefully and the footboard across the buffers to provide some form of standing space when cleaning the smokebox is visible. *K.R. Bloxham collection*

Rear cover:
Former Hastings line composite No. 5600 renumbered in November 1962 as DS70155. This was the replacement Engineer's inspection saloon for DS1. This coach was built in January 1931 to Diagram 2304 – one of only ten restriction 0 composite coaches,— and for much of its life ran as a loose vehicle. Withdrawn in September 1959, the coach was stored until entering Eastleigh Works for rebuilding during 1962. It is seen awaiting the right away from Tulse Hill station on 31 March 1969, in company with BR standard Mk 1 corridor 1st S13007 – one of few such coaches allocated to the Southern Region. This is to BR Diagram 116 and was built at Swindon in 1951. The motive power at the rear is probably a class 33 diesel or a class 73 EDL. Departmental Diagram 1958 was allocated to the inspection coach and this shows it to have a large saloon at one end (the far end in the picture) with six bucket seats in two rows of three overlooking the track, a long central table with 12 further seats, then a lavatory, a kitchen and a guard's brake compartment all connected by a side corridor (on the far side in this instance) and at the nearer end a smaller saloon, this time just with three bucket seats overlooking the track and a smaller central table with seats for six further persons. The coach has now acquired yellow end warning panels but was later painted rail blue with full yellow ends. It was often used as a route learning saloon and was withdrawn in October 1988, being sold to the Kent & East Sussex Railway. However little restoration was carried out and some fire damage occurred. In 2008 it was sold again and moved to Rampart Engineering, Derby, for restoration. However, in 2013 the coach was noted stored at Wishaw with no sign of any restoration having taken place. *Mike King*

Title page:
Pullman camping coach P45 in use at Lyndhurst Road. In reality perhaps a bit noisy with trains passing on a regular basis to and from Bournemouth, but certainly ideal for access to the New Forest. *K.R. Bloxham collection*

Contents

Introduction

Looking back over what is now 14 years, topics for the Introduction to SW have been many and various. We have spoken of the content within the present issue, future intentions, the odd rant (from me that is), pleas and requests, as well as being able to include some excellent 'Guest Editorials'. Indeed, although I have not mentioned such for a time, that position is still open. Remuneration I regret is nil, but the opportunity is there to talk about what you like, so please get in touch if you feel so inclined.

For the editorial in this issue I am going to take as my subject two points, the first the pages devoted to the images of Dr J. L. Farmer, and the second almost an ' I spy'.

Starting with the first, and I appreciate this is in some way a repetition of what you can read on page 47, but I do think it is worth emphasising the point. For 50 years plus the collection of Dr Farmer had been lost to view. In no way do I attempt to infer blame on the family, in fact totally the opposite. Our lives are busy, and the negatives had survived but were left unseen. Thank goodness Di Jeans resurrected them as several show the type of scene that is totally lost to history. It goes to prove (again) how something seemingly innocuous, a single image or two, has in fact a considerable rarity value. Indeed, moving away from railways perhaps we may even have odd items ourselves unrelated to our own interests but that may have an interest – perhaps value even – and so could fill in the gaps in someone else's interest or indeed their family.

My second point is an 'I spy'. As Terry Wogan used to say, '...The present Mrs Robertson...' (not that I am planning a replacement) and I were sitting in the car waiting at a level crossing recently. It matters not where but it was close to a station on a line I know reasonably well and certainly one which I have images of from years past.

Observing the scene – two trains passing meant the delay in the barriers lifting involved a few minutes' wait – I was struck by what is in effect a soul-less, some might even say, cold and just about functional facility. Gone were the warm red brick buildings and associated add-on wooden huts. Gone was the signal box with its wonky stove pipe chimney. Gone were the signals, the sidings, the wooden notice boards but most of all, gone were the staff. Fortunately not so the passengers, there were a few waiting for what I know was an hourly stopping train service in each direction (much of the traffic being fast express workings) and stone traffic. The latter may give a clue but it really does not matter where, it is the point of what I am recounting that matters.

On the platform were clinically painted yellow lines, a box with two buttons marked 'Help Point' whilst elsewhere was tactile paving. It all pointed towards 'do it yourself' or 'don't do this' and 'you must do that'. Oh, and a notice warning me of the dire consequences if I trespassed. Today it could cost me £1,000; a bit more than the previous forty shillings.

For one brief moment I actually had the thought perhaps this is indeed no longer a railway station. Perhaps it has now migrated to that awful term of a train station, after all do we not have coach stations not road stations? But then the need for economy has been paramount on the railway in past decades. It must pay its way, never mind about passengers any more – sorry customers.

I appreciate finding an individual prepared to truly represent the railway when left to his own devices at an isolated location is not easy. The life of a country porter in the 21st century (although I doubt there are such grades on the railway these days anyway) is hardly a role likely to appeal to many. Even if it did I imagine the turnover would probably also be on the high side.

No doubt this otherwise lack of 'ownership' is one of the reasons why various support and 'friends of (whatever) station' bands have appeared in recent years. They need our support as well. Perhaps I should consider starting one myself for what is in effect almost my local station.

Kevin Robertson

Deep in the Cornish countryside, Well Tank No. 30587 is engaged in shunting at Penpont on the Wenford Bridge branch. *K.R. Bloxham collection*

Down to Earth Part 5
Southern Stock and the Minor Companies

Mike King

Isle of Wight Railway 3-compartment composite No. 38 – one of the 40 vehicles built new for the railway between 1864 and 1882 by the Oldbury Carriage & Wagon Company of Birmingham, seen when returned to Haven Street in July 1976. These were typical 4-wheeled Oldbury products of the era and differed from later coaches in many respects – most obviously in their right-handed door hinges (the reverse of more modern stock) but also constructionally and in regard to their wheelsets and running gear – totally non-standard and unlike anything built later. The glazed toplights were also an unusual feature and were patterned blue glass (underneath that modern paint finish). This coach was one of the last two delivered new to the Island, in 1882, but was only a slightly modernised version of what had been built in 1864. It ran until March 1927, latterly becoming SR No. 6335 with one large first class compartment in the centre, flanked by two second (later third) class compartments. It was then transported to Hayling Island and built into a bungalow, where it was rediscovered in 1975 and returned to the Island a year later. Several similar coach bodies were grounded on the Isle of Wight and this one, plus a couple more of the type, still await their turn to be restored to traffic, mounted on shortened SR utility van underframes. The restoration of similar composite No. 10 was the subject of a Channel 4 documentary in 2018, but this differed in that a new purpose-built timber underframe was constructed as part of this process. *R. Newman*

We now come to those few ex-Southern Railway vintage coaches that were grounded, including electric stock, plus the minor companies. As might be expected, by the time that Southern-built vehicles were being scrapped, the demand for temporary accommodation could be met much more easily by the purchase or hire of modern pre-fabricated buildings – by the 1960s there were a number of companies specialising in such provision. I can only find a small number of Maunsell coaches so used – and not a single Bulleid or BR standard Mk. 1 vehicle seems to have been grounded. So, in this instalment we will find both the oldest and the newest grounded bodies with a few unusual sights in between, as we shall see. But first, let us look at the minor companies. With but a few exceptions, this means the Isle of Wight – ever a concentration of ancient vehicles – no matter what their origins.

Because of its geographical isolation, the Isle of Wight must contain more grounded bodies per square mile than anywhere else. Clearly, shipping in portable buildings from the mainland was expensive – and in the days before modern car ferries, difficult – so the railway was a ready source of such structures. We have already seen a few in the previous articles in the series, but all that have so far been illustrated have been former mainland company vehicles that were already second (or third) hand when they got to the Island, so by the time they were sold off and grounded, they were, most probably, on at least their fourth ownership! Who says that recycling is anything new?

Roger Silsbury compiled a list of known Island bodies and kindly sent me a copy some 40 years ago – this list amounting to no fewer than 120 vehicles of one sort or another – and despite the lapse of time several more have been discovered in the interim. They range from pre-Grouping goods vans to goods brake vans, LMS containers, Ryde Pier tramcar bodies as well as examples of almost every type of coach to run on the Island. The uses to which they were put are just as diverse: from homes to chicken huts, to pigsties, to garden sheds, to garages, to yachtsmen's stores, to cafes, to changing huts for bathers and even included a bus stop shelter at Freshwater, never mind those grounded for the railway itself – although in fact these were actually in the minority. Quite a number have been recovered by the Isle of Wight steam railway and are either already restored, in the process of restoration, or in store at Haven Street awaiting their turn in the queue. Those who remember the 2018 Channel Four TV series on carriage restoration may recall that one programme was devoted to a former Isle of Wight Railway composite coach of 1864. Currently there are at least 12 more bodies awaiting restoration – all of which have been recovered from either the Island or from Hayling – to where a few had been 'exported' around the 1924-27 period.

The narrow-gauge Lynton & Barnstaple Railway also became part of the Southern Railway's assets in 1923 and, following closure in 1935, several bodies were grounded in the vicinity of the line. No less than three were retained as chalets/summerhouses on their bogies and on short lengths of track at Snapper Halt and two have survived. One is now at the National Railway Museum at York, the other is very much rebuilt as 'The Snapper Bar' on the Festiniog Railway. Parts of several others, plus a complete bogie brake van, are also now owned by the present-day Lynton & Barnstaple Association at Woody Bay and are either restored or in the process of being incorporated into replica vehicles. Another heritage railway worth visiting to see what can be achieved from a humble starting point.

Returning to the mainland, a small number of electric stock vehicles got a further lease of life after withdrawal in the 1950s – these were mostly wooden-bodied coaches that had already seen use as four or six-wheeled steam-hauled vehicles and were rebuilt on new underframes between 1925 and 1938. The 62ft underframes, being at least a quarter-century newer, got re-used as EPB vehicles during the 1950s. The original 1898 Waterloo & City line cars were replaced in 1940 and at least 18 were dumped on the trackside at Eardley Road sidings soon after. However, given the difficulties of the time, perhaps this was simply a matter of expediency rather than being put to any sort of further use. Nevertheless, at least two were still there in 1948. Another interesting (and unique) vehicle put to further use was the Sentinel steam railcar No. 6, used as a Home Guard messroom at the back of Ashford Works.

While mentioning Ashford Works, that location gave the writer his first sight of a grounded SR utility van – No. 1154 – at the eastern end of the loco works, near Willesborough level crossing, in the late 1960s. Grounding of such vehicles became more common in the 1970s and 1980s as general withdrawal of these gathered pace. Many of these were miles away from the Southern Region, too, while others are being used at heritage railways throughout the country. In many cases the vans were purchased simply for their underframes to be utilised under much older bodies, leaving the railway with a perfectly serviceable (and authentic) lineside storeroom.

One other type of coach not noted as being grounded were ex-LSWR and SR-built 'Ironclads' – at least until more recent times! However, as reported in the 'Railway Observer', corridor third coach 760, later DW70013, was sold by scrap dealer Booth's of Rotherham in 1979 and was grounded nearby in the village of Harthill Firvale, circa 1982. However, a Google Earth search reveals no sign of it today. Those who read SW52 will also be aware of similar 'Ironclad' coach 717 now residing at Horsebridge station – but this is in one piece and rests on a short length of reconstructed track. It therefore does not quite qualify as a grounded body. Neither do the Pullman cars providing hotel accommodation at Petworth station and doubtless there are a few others that are being used similarly elsewhere.

We will finish with another selection of pictures and if you, the reader, know of a grounded body that still exists somewhere near you, I would be most interested to know about it via the editor. It could quite easily be one that I have never found! Indeed, since the series commenced, I have been advised of at least two that were previously unrecorded – another Pullman car near Selsey and an LSWR corridor composite near Three Bridges station. The Home Guard depot near Gomshall, mentioned in Part 2, turned out to be a Southern Railway-owned training site, but whether it was purely for railway staff or was hired out to other organisations is not known. One presumes that the carriage bodies grounded at this location were demolished soon after the end of the war. The Bluebell Railway acquired two more ex-SER six-wheeled bodies from Pagham in 2017 so clearly there are more out there waiting to be discovered.

HALLOWEEN

TH
261

In 1914 the Isle of Wight Railway purchased no less than 18 ex-Metropolitan Railway rigid 8-wheelers. At first sight these appear to be bogie coaches, but in fact the outer axles were allowed some lateral movement to enable them to negotiate curves. All 18 seem to have been grounded at various Island locations after withdrawal in 1928/29 and no less than nine may be seen in this view, taken at St Helens Duver in the early 1950s. They were used as changing huts for bathers and proved ideal for this purpose. When last seen by the author about 15 years ago, they had been clad in shiplap timbers. A recent Google Earth search reveals that some, at least, remain there today. Two types may be identified – a 6-compartment first (composite or third on the Island) and 8-compartment third, but there were several other variants amongst the 18 examples, including a few with 7 compartments. They became IWR numbers 5-9, 14-17, 21-23, 29-32 and 35/36 – later SR thirds 2432-2440 and composites 6338-6346. Latterly they were formed in Ryde-Ventnor sets 485-487 (six each) with ex-LSWR vans at each end until withdrawal in 1928/29. As 'people-shifters' they were ideal for this route, but not surprisingly the Southern did not share the Isle of Wight company's enthusiasm for them and they were soon earmarked for early replacement. Identification of the nine at St Helens proved difficult, as they had been repainted so many times since grounding that all traces of former identity had been lost. *R. J. C. Day*

Opposite top: An ex-North London Railway coach, this was IWR composite No. 46 and also seen at Haven Street in July 1976, after arrival from Hayling Island where it had been since withdrawal in 1926. There it was also built into a bungalow, named 'Halloween'. Built probably at Bow Works for London suburban services sometime in 1864, it was one of eleven coaches purchased second-hand from the North London Railway in 1897/98. It was 27ft long and was a 4-wheeled, 4-compartment first, but was reclassified as a composite, with one end compartment demoted to second, later third class, soon after arrival on the island. It was returned to service in 1986, mounted on a shortened former utility van underframe and was at first finished in IWR teak livery, but has since been repainted in Southern lined olive green, carrying its SR number of 6336. *R. Newman*

Bottom: Isle of Wight Central Railway guards van No. 17, seen grounded at Newport on 29 March 1948. This was allocated the SR number 990 in the van list but never carried it – instead being withdrawn in March 1927 and transferred to departmental stock as No. 427s in September 1929. It was finally withdrawn from departmental duties in 1938 and grounded as seen in 1939. In fact, it retained its four 'W' irons and sat some 3ft above ground level – being used as a store. Dimensions were 21ft long and 7ft 10in wide over body, but the lookouts must have added perhaps another 12 inches in width. Its exact origins are unknown, but the vertical matchboarding all round was practically unique on the Island. How long it remained at Newport is not known. *J. H. Aston*

An 8-compartment vehicle, IWR No. 5 (SR third 2432), again at St Helens, but a little further north on The Duver and standing on its own, also used as a changing hut. All four of the 8-compartment - 80 seat vehicles were grounded at St Helens, so in this and the previous photograph, all four are just visible. Dimensionally, they were all 39ft 6in long and 8ft 2in wide over bodywork. However, IWR No. 9 (SR composite 6338) had a first class coupe (half-compartment) with end windows at one end with seven other third class compartments, while No. 15 (SR 6340) was unique in having flat-topped doors. The picture dates from 26 June 1950. *D. Cullum*

Opposite top: Also at St Helens on 26 June 1950 was 6-compartment composite SR 6346 (ex-IWR No. 36), now going under the name of 'Merryways'! This was configured 111333 but some of the other six-compartment coaches had just two firsts and four thirds while others had been downgraded to all-third class. The seven-compartment vehicles were fitted out as 3311333, or 7x 3rd, so there was plenty of scope for variety amongst the 18 coaches and this would have been even greater prior to 1923 when second class was also provided for. The Metropolitan Railway scrapped or sold off most of these rigid 8-wheelers in the early years of the 20th Century (they dated from 1863-1884) and their last survivors ran on the Brill branch in Buckinghamshire until it closed in 1935. *D. Cullum*

Bottom: Of the 17 ex-Lynton & Barnstaple Railway coaches, three were sold off (for just £10 each) and remained on short lengths of the track at Snapper Halt, just outside Barnstaple, after the line closed in 1935, serving as summerhouses. This is No. 15, seen semi-derelict in 1956 and by then being used as a henhouse! Two such 5-compartment brake thirds were built for the line in 1898 by the Bristol Wagon & Carriage Company, numbered 15 and 16. No. 16 remained as a brake third and became SR No. 4108 while No. 15 was altered to a brake composite in 1903, becoming SR No. 6993. After standing at Snapper for some 24 years it was rescued by the Ffestiniog Railway and taken to Boston Lodge Works in 1959. There it was much rebuilt and now serves as their coach No. 14, named 'The Snapper Bar'. Portions of several other coach bodies were also grounded in North Devon and the present-day Lynton & Barnstaple Association has acquired them with a view to incorporating the parts into replica vehicles for use on the preservation line at Woody Bay. To date five have been reconstructed – plus a bogie brake van. *J. E. Hoyland*

MERRYWAYS

One of the other coaches at Snapper, L&BR No. 1/SR No. 6991, was a brake composite complete with observation saloon (the section nearest the camera) in this 1936 picture. Also visible are the 'Lot 17' paint marks indicating the recent sale, which took place at Pilton Works, Barnstaple, on 13 November 1935. The coach resided at Snapper for a number of years before being transported to Clannaborough Rectory, near Copplestone, again to be used as a summerhouse. It is reputed that several church meetings were then held in the coach! It was finally acquired by the National Railway Museum in 1982, where it is on public view – albeit not yet restored. *L & GRP*

Below: A relatively small number of former electric stock vehicles were grounded – the most common being former 2-coach trailer set SECR or LBSCR vehicles – one of the latter was illustrated in Part 3. However, here we have a former SECR 3-SUB composite coach, No. 9561, grounded in a quiet corner of Lancing Works yard. This was to SR Diagram 754 – a nine-compartment vehicle that ran originally as the centre coach in 3-car unit 1468 and later in 4-SUB unit 4478. However, the body started life as two ex-SER 27ft 4-wheeled steam-hauled suburban 4-compartment composites – SECR Nos. 283 and 285 and these were built by Gloucester RCW Co. in 1898 – part of a large order for eleven 8-coach trains. Latterly the pair ran in SECR close-coupled suburban 6-set No. 302, from 1914 until withdrawn in 1925. They were then taken and mounted at each end of a new 62ft underframe and an additional compartment spliced into the gap in the centre to make up the nine compartments. Each end compartment was fitted out as third class, the rest were first class and the coach took its place in unit 1468, between similarly rebuilt motor brake thirds 8361/62. From October 1941 the unit lost its first class accommodation (in line with all SR suburban services) owing to wartime conditions. In January 1947 the unit was augmented by a Bulleid all-steel trailer coach (at first No. 10269, later 10259) – which clearly stuck out like a sore thumb against the ex-SECR bodywork of the other three vehicles! However, this formation was not maintained for very long as the Bulleid coach was soon replaced in April 1950 by another SECR vehicle – identical trailer composite (now third) 9558. In this form the unit lasted just another year before withdrawal in June 1951. Such were the many changes suffered by suburban electric units. The body of coach 9561 then came to rest as seen and remained there for at least 10 years.
Dr T. Gough/Transport Treasury

Very few Maunsell coaches were grounded – and the author has only ever noted nine in just five locations. Three coaches were grounded on the embankment north of New Cross Gate (thirds 1143 and 1152, plus brake third 2802), three at Eastleigh (open third 1376 and unclassed open saloons 7964/83) and one each at Lancing (open third 1332), Newhaven and Horsham. Two Restriction 1 'Thanet' coaches were so used at the latter locations – composite 5542 at Newhaven and third 981, seen here at Horsham in the early 1960s and serving as a messroom. Both coaches were withdrawn in 1959 when phase 1 of the Kent Coast electrification caused a sudden surplus of steam-hauled carriage stock. Coach 981 was to SR Diagram 53 and had originally been destined for Chichester, but was dispatched to Horsham instead. Why the change of plan is not known, but Chichester received a standard Restriction 4 Maunsell corridor first instead – but still on its wheels. No. 5542 at Newhaven stood on its wheels on the dockside for some time before succumbing to gravity. Most of the coaches listed above remained on site until the early 1970s. *Dr T. Gough/Transport Treasury*

Both the grounded unclassed open saloon vehicles to Diagram 2653 at Eastleigh in the early 1960s. Coach 7964 is seen in the carriage works yard, while 7983 occupies a space alongside the locomotive works. Both had been grounded about 1960. Restriction 4 open third 1376 was also grounded within the carriage works but under cover and was still there after the works closed. A total of 62 'general saloons' to Diagram 2653 were completed between 1928 and 1931 for race, boat and school-party traffic. Essentially they had seating of almost first-class standard arranged in seven open bays with a lavatory at each end, alternate bays having access doors. Some were soon permanently marked as second class – at a time when the Southern catered very little for this class of traffic – but if one was lucky enough to travel in a coach while holding a third class ticket, then the ride would be a most comfortable one! Some similar brake vehicles were built in 1933 and, like the general saloons, were mostly to be found on boat trains. However, by the mid-1950s some had gravitated to ordinary services and the writer travelled in one between Redhill and Guildford, not long before the last was withdrawn in 1964, and recalls the comfortable brown cord upholstery. *Dr T. Gough/Transport Treasury*

Sentinel railcar No. 6, still on wheels and just about on rails, dumped at the back of Ashford Works yard and seen on 20 April 1949. It had been used as a Home Guard hut during the war. This was ordered in 1932, partly as an experiment to find more economical ways to operate certain unremunerative branch lines. Drewry railcar No. 5 had been obtained some five years earlier for similar purposes. The Sentinel car was tried on The Dyke branch from 1 May 1933 – a short but steeply graded line which saw little regular patronage except for recreational purposes on Summer Saturday afternoons and Sundays – when a loco-hauled train was used instead. Some success was achieved and so the purchase of five more was authorised – not that the unit saved The Dyke branch as this closed on 1 January 1939! The car was also used on the Westerham branch and on other services radiating from Tonbridge. No. 6 eventually suffered a catastrophic failure on Colebrook Viaduct, near Tunbridge Wells, on 22 April 1937, which caused havoc to all services in the area. It eventually reached Ashford Works for repair and was intended for further trials on the Gravesend West branch, but instead failed a boiler examination and was condemned in January 1942, having never turned a wheel again. Better use was made of it as a Home Guard messroom. It was finally broken up later in 1949. *J. H. Aston*

The Waterloo & City line opened as a nominally independent concern in 1898 and the rolling stock was of a rather unorthodox design, supplied by the American firm of Jackson Sharp and Company and by Dick, Kerr of Preston. A few additional vehicles were completed later at Eastleigh but resembled the originals very closely. By the late 1930s they were overdue for replacement and new Bulleid-designed vehicles were supplied during 1940. The original cars were then brought to the surface in October 1940 and no less than 18 were dumped on the trackside at Eardley Road sidings, Streatham. However, this may simply have been expedient rather than them being put to any form of further use. However, at least two bodyshells, together with their underframes, remained on site in July 1948, when they were photographed. These are, on the right, single unit motor No. 14, built by Dick, Kerr & Co., and beyond, trailer car 36, built at Eastleigh in 1922. Denis Cullum recorded that, on 30 September 1946, no less than ten were visible here – Nos. 1, 5, 10, 14, 15, 24, 25, 26, 30 and 36. Presumably, by 1948 the rest had been broken up. *J. H. Meredith*

Christmas Mails and Parcels Traffic
A Retrospective Review Part 2

Richard Simmons

With regard to services starting from Battersea, the P notice gives no information as to where in the Battersea complex this relates to: presumably it was from the former GWR (sorry to have to refer to this 'other' railway in the hallowed pages of SW! but needs be) goods depot at South Lambeth which was transferred to the Southern Region. P notice timings do not even show passing times at Longhedge Junction. Two empty van trains for these services departed Clapham Junction at 7.30am (EWD) and 6.30pm (EWD) both formed of 23 vans – no particular type being specified- so presumably Clapham Junction utilised whatever happened to be on hand, but the 7.30am had to include one van B (stove) and the 6.30pm one brake. A specific note in the P notice stated that neither train could be cancelled except by prior arrangement with Waterloo HO; I wonder why? Furthermore, the P notice also charged Clapham Junction to forward two spare tail lamps to Battersea on the 7.30am. A unique situation in these days of electric tail lamps.

At Wimbledon the Volunteer Siding was located next to the up Local (now up Slow Line) and trailing into that line at the Raynes Park end of the station. The siding no longer exists, but there was a platform alongside it and amongst undergrowth in parts it is still possible to discern some of the platform face. It would not have been an easy movement to arrange for the Battersea vans to be transferred from the West Yard to the siding, as it was necessary to cross the Sutton lines, down Local and Through lines (now down Slow and Fast lines), up Through (now up Fast) line on to the up Local (now up Slow) line and run into the station platform then propel back into the Volunteer siding.

Unusual shunting power at Salisbury in the form of 'Schools' No. 30913 *Christ's Hospital*.

Woking-Alton and Portsmouth

11.45 (EWD)/8.25pm/9.50pm (Su)/11.48pm (EWD) Woking-Portsmouth & Southsea. 12.19am (EWD)/12.15pm (Su)/12.48pm (EWD)/8.20pm (EWD)/9.13pm (Su) Woking-Alton 9.36am (EWD) Portsmouth & Southsea-Walton

10.30pm (EWD) Portsmouth Harbour-Nine Elms "J" Shed (EWD = every weekday)

10.5pm (EWD) Alton-Woking

Weybridge & Walton to Nine Elms "J" Shed

2.10am (Mondays only) Weybridge-Walton

5.0am (EWD)/10.5am (EWD)/2.35pm (EWD) Walton-Nine Elms "J" Shed

7.32pm (EWD) Wimbledon Volunteer Siding-Clapham Junction via East Putney

Salisbury-Portsmouth

2.25am (EWD & Su)Salisbury-Portsmouth & Southsea via Eastleigh

3.5pm (EWD) Salisbury-Portsmouth & Southsea via Southampton Terminus and Netley 9.15pm (EWD)/9.35pm (Su) Portsmouth & Southsea- Salisbury via Eastleigh

10.3pm (EWD) Portsmouth & Southsea-Walton via Eastleigh

Salisbury-Westbury

4.30am (EWD) Salisbury-Bristol (Temple Meads) 9.0pm (EWD) Bristol Temple Meads-Salisbury

Waterloo-West of England

12.23am & 10.50pm (both EWD) Exeter Central-Exeter St Davids (vans off down services)

12.40am (various dates) Salisbury-Exeter Central 9.0am (EWD) Yeovil Junction-Yeovil Town

1.10pm (Su) Exeter Central-Torrington (also conveyed fish)

6.35pm (Su) Waterloo-Basingstoke (vans for West of England)

6.42pm (EWD) Waterloo-Exeter Central (non-stop Salisbury-Exeter Central)

4.15pm (Su) Torrington-Templecombe (conveyed milk empties and parcels)

7.50pm (EWD) Launceston-Crediton (attached at Crediton to 9.10pm ex-Barnstaple Junction)

8.25pm (various dates) Exeter Central-Walton

9.10pm (EWD) Barnstaple Junction-Exeter Central

Waterloo-Reading

10.50am & 11.53am (various dates)/4.58pm (Su)/8.10pm (EWD) Waterloo-Reading South via Hounslow

10.38pm (EWD) Hounslow-Nine Elms "J" Shed via Twickenham

Reading-Guildford-Redhill

5.22am (EWD/2.3pm (Su)/6.5pmEWD) Reading South-Redhill

6.10am (EWD & Su) Redhill-Reading South

In addition Reading South had to provide additional vans as necessary next to the engine of trains to Redhill for Brighton and other destinations in the Sussex coastal area advising full details to Woking Trains Supervision Office.

Waterloo-Richmond via Kingston and also via Teddington

11.11am (Sa)/12.38pm (EWD)/5.40pm (Su)/8.32pm (EWD) Waterloo-Richmond via Kingston and Twickenham

5.37pm (EWD) Shepperton-Hounslow via Kingston (reverse) and Twickenham (reverse)

Christmas Day

The following special van trains ran:

12.15am and 4.0am Eastleigh-Southampton Terminus

5.22am Reading South-Redhill

10.30am Waterloo-Clapham Junction via Brentford Central and Twickenham

Electric Parcels Trains Conveying Parcels and Parcels Post

These were formed of 8 cars, 2x4-SUB units, which operated as follows:

10.49(EWD & Sa 3.44pm Su) Waterloo-Wimbledon via Worcester Park, Effingham Junction, Guildford (reverse), Effingham Junction, Cobham and Surbiton.

4.14pm (EWD) Waterloo-Wimbledon non-stop via Cobham to Effingham Junction where the train divided. Front unit returned to Wimbledon via Leatherhead and Epsom, rear unit returned to Wimbledon via Cobham.

4.14pm (Sa) Waterloo-Wimbledon non-stop via Cobham to Effingham Junction where the train divided. Front unit returned to Wimbledon via Cobham, rear unit returned to Wimbledon via Leatherhead and Epsom. The P notice instructed Waterloo to provide 2 men (sic) to travel on these trains to assist with parcels traffic.

Alfred Road

This item under the vans category raises a conundrum, relating to vans of parcels post from Alfred Road (WR) to Reading South. Four vans of this traffic were booked to arrive at Reading General twice during every evening whilst the P notice operated, being available for transfer to Reading South approximately one hour later. But the conundrum is where is

No. 75068 leaving Southampton with the 11.38am Basingstoke to Southampton Western Docks van train.

the location of Alfred Road? Finding no record of any station or depot of this name I referred to 'County Street Atlas Berkshire' (Philips 1990), and 'The Railway Clearing House Handbook of Railway Stations 1904' in an attempt to establish if there is, or was, a street/road with this name thus indicating a GPO sorting office on such a thoroughfare which could have a railway connection, but with no success. *Can any reader help with further information?* (There is an Alfred STREET in central Reading – it's about three furlongs from Reading station and is now, apparently, part of the A329, running just north of the old Oxford Road where it left central Reading – courtesy Alastair Wilson.)

Isle of Wight

The Island did get a brief mention with a few items for Sunday 21 December and Christmas Day. There were additional ferry sailings from Portsmouth Harbour to Ryde Pier departing from Portsmouth at 2.50am on 21 December and 3.10am on Christmas Day. These connected with additional trains from Ryde Pier Head at 4.0am and 4.5am to Cowes and Ventnor respectively which ran to weekdays timings. But what was, perhaps, a surprise additional service was a 4.50am Newport to Freshwater which also ran to weekdays timings so this too, must have been a regular working. The Cowes and Ventnor trains returned empty to Ryde St. Johns Road but the Freshwater train for some unknown reason only returned empty to Newport on Christmas Day, presumably on 21 December the engine returned light as far as Newport MPD.

1953 Notice P71 LWD 1953 from Monday 14 to Saturday 26 December (Inclusive)

Additional to those trains listed for 1952 were the following:

7.0am (EWD) Waterloo-Weymouth

5.25pm (Su) Battersea -Woking via East Putney which made an if required stop at Wimbledon Park to detach assisting engine. Presumably this additional motive power was required for the adverse gradients from Latchmere Junction to Clapham Junction and Point Pleasant Junction to East Putney. 11.30pm (EWD) Eastleigh to Southampton Terminus.

For the 5.5pm Bournemouth West-Waterloo, Bournemouth West had to ensure the booked van was a bogie vehicle into which all letter mail traffic had to be loaded. Stations had to ensure all such traffic was loaded into this vehicle for which an Assisting Guard had to be provided to supervise loading and sorting thereof.

Former LSWR 44' Passenger Guards Van No. 1015 at Newport.

Weybridge and Walton to Nine Elms

4.0am and 5.0am (Su) Walton-Nine Elms "A" signal box thence to "J" Shed via North and South Viaduct signal boxes.

Waterloo-West of England

7.50pm (EWD) Launceston-Crediton terminate Yeoford where vans attached to 9.10pm ex-Barnstaple Junction-Exeter Central.

Waterloo-Richmond via Kingston

5.37pm (EWD) Shepperton-Hounslow via Kingston (reverse) and Twickenham (reverse) terminate Twickenham.

10.38pm (EWD) Hounslow-Nine Elms "J" Shed, on Saturdays run to Nine Elms "A" signal box thence to "J" Shed via North and South Viaduct signal boxes at 1.5am Sundays.

Isle of Wight

On Christmas Day morning additional boat 3.10am Portsmouth Harbour-Ryde Pier connecting into 4.0am and 4.5am additional trains to Cowes and Ventnor respectively running to weekday timings, with no reference to consequential return empty stock trains. An error was the continued inclusion of the 4.50am Newport-Freshwater as the Freshwater branch had closed on 21 September 1953! Doubtless a correction was made later.

Christmas Day

The following additional van trains ran:

2.25am Salisbury-Portsmouth & Southsea via Eastleigh 3.55am Eastleigh-Southampton Terminus 5.22am Reading South-Guildford 10.30am Waterloo-Clapham Junction via Brentford Central and Twickenham for which Waterloo had to provide vans as required 1.0pm Waterloo-Clapham Junction (Kensington Sidings).

To finish our 1953 review just a couple of items to illustrate that through routes now long disappeared also did their bit to convey Christmas mails.

Somerset and Dorset

On the 6.40pm Bournemouth West-Bath, Bournemouth West had to provide a van (type unspecified) formed next to the train set labelled "BATH" for letter mails from Bournemouth West only for destinations in the Midlands and North.

Midland & South Western Junction Railway

On the 4.36pm Southampton Terminus-Cheltenham Spa (Lansdown) there was a daily van to Cheltenham which continued through to Birmingham (New Street) to convey parcels post and parcels. Also conveyed was a second van to Birmingham (New Street) for letter mail only from Southampton Terminus for destinations via Cheltenham in the Midlands, North-East, North West England and Scotland.

1956 Notice No. P.95. L.W.D. 1956 From Thursday 13 to Wednesday 26 December (inclusive), 69 pages

Signal Box Opening Hours

The following signal boxes were shown in addition to those in the 1952 listing: Dinton, Hewish Siding, Hinton Admiral, Meldon Junction, Porton, Seaton Junction, Semley, Shawford Junction, Swaythling and Wootton.

Staple motive power on the Island during the final years of steam were the O2 class, represented here by No. W30 *Shorwell* arriving at Wroxall on a Ryde Pier Head to Ventnor train.

Additional Instruction Ice Cream Empties

All Messrs. Walls, I.C.I. and Eldorado empty containers together with empties for Messrs. J. Lyons & Co had to be despatched to Nine Elms for direct cartage to premises of Firms concerned.

Van Inspection

All vans received as 'empty' or on terminating journeys had to be thoroughly examined to ensure all traffic had been cleared. Station Masters and Supervisors were instructed to give this matter special attention.

Ocean Mails Ex-Southampton Docks for London

Were dealt with at Nine Elms (Brunswick Yard) and had to be loaded in 4-wheeled vanfits. Freight traffic permitting, all available loaded vanfits with this traffic had to be forwarded next engine of the 6.55pm (Freight) Southampton Old (now Eastern) Docks-Nine Elms and remainder – if any – forwarded by the 8.4pm (Parcels) Southampton Old Docks-Crewe for probable transfer at Eastleigh or Basingstoke but this was not made clear in the P notice.

Shunting Engines

Locations added were Clapham Yard, Southampton Central and Bournemouth Central. Meanwhile Ash was deleted.

Additional Van Trains

Main Line 6.0am (EWD & Su) Nine Elms Empties Shed-Bournemouth Central

7.0am (Su) Waterloo-Woking

2.10pm (Su) Nine Elms Empties Shed-Clapham Yard

2.20pm (EWD) Nine Elms Empties Shed-Woking 4.20pm (EWD) Bournemouth Central -Walton 10.03pm (EWD) Portsmouth & Southsea-Walton via Eastleigh

Portsmouth Direct Line

10.38am (EWD) Guildford-Woking

8.20pm (EWD) Godalming Goods-Guildford

10.30pm (EWD) Portsmouth Harbour-Nine Elms "J" Shed via Guildford

10.38pm (EWD) Fratton-Guildford

The 11.23pm Portsmouth & Southsea-Eastleigh passenger and van train included vans for Bristol, Waterloo, Bournemouth Central and Plymouth, conveying traffic for destinations over large areas of the country, vans being forwarded from Eastleigh by ordinary services. Clearly it was essential that none of the connecting services were missed and to this effect, the P notice included an instruction stating the train had to start to time and not be held at Fratton for connection with the 9.50pm Waterloo-Portsmouth Harbour. In the event of the connection being severed, an additional 11.35pm Q service Portsmouth & Southsea-Fareham was shown in the P notice which was to run in the event of there being passengers off the 9.50pm ex-Waterloo for Cosham, Portchester or Fareham. It would be interesting to know on how many occasions the train ran – if at all. The ECS returned to Fratton.

A major ingredient of both passenger and parcels traffic to the Isle of Wight was the ferry service, represented here with M V *Brading* arriving at Ryde from Portsmouth.

Isle of Wight

Additional sailings from Portsmouth Harbour to Ryde Pier at 2.50am and 3.10am on 23 December and 25 December respectively, with on both mornings additional trains at 4.0am and 4.5am from Ryde Pier Head to Cowes and Ventnor respectively.

Following timing columns for individual special parcels trains, came their formations and no less than 93 separate service details for vans, usually one or sometimes two on scheduled service trains. Obviously this number means it is impossible to quote details for each individual van, but I think some reference should be made to the 'Withered Arm' section, ie west of Exeter, because by now there must be very few former Southern Region staff remaining who can recall, or even write down, details of working practices on what was Southern Region territory. Unless something is recorded details could be lost for ever. So here goes!

Additional vans worked to and from Bideford, Bude, Callington, Exmouth, Ilfracombe, Plymouth Friary, Sidmouth, Torrington and Yeovil Town: a sobering thought that out of that list only Exmouth remains today. The last up departure of the day northwards from Padstow was as early as 6.0pm to Okehampton and in both summer and winter months, must have been too early for the last collection from many pillar boxes which was likely to have been around 8.0pm. Noteworthy in that train's formation, however, was an additional Van B for Exeter Central in which amongst parcels and mail traffic space was reserved for – wait for it – rabbit traffic (presumably deceased!). Where these unfortunate animals were loaded or unloaded was not recorded, but was this practice of conveying rabbits by rail peculiar to the West Country?

The following special van trains ran on Christmas Day:

12.20am Woking-Portsmouth & Southsea

12.48am Woking-Alton

2.25am Salisbury-Eastleigh

3.55am Eastleigh-Southampton Terminus

5.25am Reading South-Guildford

11.30am Waterloo-Clapham Junction via Brentford Central and Twickenham

1.0pm Waterloo-Clapham Junction (Kensington Sidings)

No freight train revisions were included.

Moving on to following years, only principal alterations to the 1952 pattern will be noted. Additional Opening of Signal Boxes. Add Winchester Junction.

Additional Shunting Engines

As a reminder of where these were provided, in 1956 these worked at the following locations: Waterloo (continuously from 6.0am Thursday 13 December until Noon Christmas Day), Nine Elms (Hay Yard), Clapham Yard, Woking, Hounslow, Portsmouth & Southsea (continuously as at Waterloo), Aldershot, Guildford, Basingstoke, Eastleigh, Southampton Terminus, Southampton Central, Bournemouth Central, Salisbury (normal coaching shunting arrangements withdrawn and replaced by two engines), Barnstaple Junction and Reading South.

Special Services. During the 'missing years' (1954 and 1955) for which I do not have P notices, use of Battersea Yard ceased and seemed to have been replaced by Nine Elms Empties Shed. An interesting introduction marking the advent of BR Standard Mk 1 stock was that the 3.5pm Bournemouth West-Waterloo was to be provided with a BR Standard 3 set with large brake ends vice a Bulleid 770 type set.

1957 Supplementary Notice No. P.104 L.W.D. 1957 operative Saturday 14 to Thursday 26 December (inclusive) 69 pages

Additional opening of Signal Boxes. To 1956 list add Bow and delete Meldon Junction.

Additional shunting engines. To 1956 list add Millbrook.

Special Services

Due to late delivery of new diesel units, the Hampshire Diesel Scheme was only partially introduced on 16 September 1957 with the full introduction just less than two months later on 4 November 1957. Several additional van trains were timetabled from 16 September to compensate for the withdrawal of steam services with their ability to also include vans of parcels, etc. Nevertheless during the 1957 Christmas parcels period, a number of diesel and electric services which normally terminated and started from Portsmouth & Southsea ran to and from Portsmouth Harbour to ease platform occupation at Portsmouth & Southsea low level platforms.

Isle of Wight

Additional boats 2.50am (Sunday 22 / 3.10am (Christmas Day)) Portsmouth Harbour-Ryde Pier connecting into 4.0am and 4.5am Ryde Pier Head to Cowes and Ventnor respectively.

Christmas Day

The following additional van trains ran:

12.20am Woking-Portsmouth & Southsea

12.48am Woking-Alton

3.10am Clapham Yard-Portsmouth & Southsea via Eastleigh

3.55am Eastleigh-Southampton Terminus

6.30am Woking-Alton

11.30am Waterloo-Clapham Junction via Brentford Central and Twickenham

1.0pm Waterloo-Clapham Junction (Kensington Sidings)

5.25am Reading South-Guildford

M7s Nos. 30030 and 30029 leaving Southampton Central in charge of the 4.07pm Waterloo – Marchwood Military siding service. The engine(s) for this train would have been changed at Southampton Central.

Mixed traction on the Mid Hants line. Class 33 D6549 and No. 34025 *Whimple* on the diverted 09.33 Waterloo – Bournemouth Central. Assuming there was no defect with the steam engine, diesel assistance would be provided from Alton up the steep climb to Medstead although it seemed to vary where the assisting loco was detached.

1958 Supplementary Notice from Monday 15 to Friday 26 December (inclusive) 72 pages

Additional Signal Box openings and additional Shunting Engines. In 1957 the P notice listed 23 boxes with additional opening hours and 1958 saw a reduction of three with Hewish Siding, Sutton Bingham and Winchester Junction disappearing. Additional shunting engines were provided at the same locations as 1957.

An interesting item concerned the 4.25pm Southampton Terminus-Andover Junction via Eastleigh which at the inception of the Hampshire Diesel Scheme started life as a DEW, but became one of a number of services temporarily replaced by steam trains between 15 September 1958 and 2 January 1960 to ease maintenance problems with the DEMUs. In the 1958 Christmas mails and parcels period, use was made of the steam traction on this train to convey an additional (sealed) van on the rear for Birmingham Snow Hill, for letter mail only from Southampton Terminus to destinations in the Midlands, North-East, North-West England and Scotland. The van was, however, interestingly routed via the Didcot, Newbury and Southampton Railway – then not yet closed – by Eastleigh transferring it to the 5.12pm service from Eastleigh to Didcot which, in fact, Saturdays excepted, started from Southampton Terminus! Otherwise there were only minor alterations to the 1957 service pattern.

Christmas Day

The same additional van trains ran as in 1957 plus a 2.30am Waterloo-Clapham Yard.

1959 (Supplemental), Notice No. P.82 1.(W.)D. 1959. From Monday 14 to Saturday 26 December (inclusive) 69 pages

Additional opening of signal boxes. Add Branksome, Grimstone and Frampton (by now in SR territory following regional transfer from the WR in 1958), Horsley and Sway.

A stand-by train, together with Motorman and Guard, to be available at Waterloo to work to Alton and Portsmouth & Southsea as required between 11.0am and 4.0pm.

Channel Islands traffic. Details were given of sailings from Weymouth Quay and Southampton Old Docks to Guernsey and Jersey, together with latest train departures from Waterloo which could be used and latest arrival times at Weymouth and Southampton. By then the Southern Region was responsible for all Channel Islands sailings.

16 Additional shunting engines; add Kew Bridge South.

An interesting situation came to light west of Exeter. Shown in the Freight WTT was a weekdays 2.6am (Freight and Mails) Exeter Central-Torrington which included a PMV(4) and BY Stove for Plymouth, a Van B and Goods brake van for Bude and a Goods brake van for Halwill. By which services these particular vehicles reached their respective destinations the P notice does not divulge, I suspect that information was apparent in the Freight WTT. With Christmas Day 1959 falling on a Saturday, together with other freight services, this train would not have run so had to be shown in the P notice as running – which it did. Also arrangements had to be made for the Plymouth and Bude vans but the Plymouth van only appeared to be conveying traffic as far as Tavistock North. This was done by the 3.35am Yeoford-Tavistock North and 4.37am Okehampton-Bude running to timings shown in the Freight WTT. The Tavistock North van continued as an empty train at 5.0am on to Plymouth Friary, but the Bude van remained at that resort with the engine returning light to Okehampton. The 'withered arm' was not dead yet!

Inwards Mail and Parcels Bags for Bordon

Additional van trains 8.15am Portsmouth Southsea-Salisbury via Southampton Terminus where it reposed from 9.45am until 12.58pm to make use of a booked light engine from Southampton Terminus to Salisbury. Nevertheless it was a lightweight train, a brake van for Salisbury and a van for Eastleigh transferred at Southampton Terminus to a service on to Eastleigh and that seemed to be all!

4.10pm (18, 19, 21 and 22 December only) Bournemouth Central to Walton-on-Thames via Southampton Terminus Yard. Unusual in that this train was not shown to run to any actual platforms at Southampton Terminus. From the P notice it can be deduced that this was to facilitate transfer of vans via Banbury and other destinations in what was then the Western Region plus Crewe and transfer, by a 7.0pm trip to Southampton Old Docks, for inclusion in the 8.20pm parcels Southampton Old Docks-Crewe.

4.35pmSX Southampton Terminus-Millbrook

6.35pmSO Southampton Old Docks-Millbrook

6.40pm (Su) Millbrook-Walton-on-Thames

9.25pm (EWD) Millbrook-Basingstoke North Yard (this being the ex-GWR yard)

Noticeable this year that Walton was given its full title of Walton-on-Thames.

The complicated arrangement at Templecombe which would see stopping Somerset and Dorset passenger trains either run in and then be assisted out, or in the opposite direction the reverse applied. Here Class 5 No. 73052 arrives southbound with the 4.52pm Evercreech Junction to Bournemouth West working, 15 June 1963.

Additional electric parcels, 9.1am, 12.4pm and 8.4pm (all EWD) and 11.38am (Su) Guildford-Sutton, returning from Sutton at 11.0am, 1.1pm and 9.0pm (all EWD) and 1.6pm (Su), all carrying headcode 29.

Isle of Wight

Christmas Day only 3.10am additional sailing Portsmouth Harbour-Ryde Pier connecting into 4.0am and 4.5am additional trains Ryde Pier Head-Cowes and Ventnor respectively.

Christmas Day

In addition to the West Country services already referred to, those listed for 1957 also ran plus the 2.30am Waterloo-Clapham Yard.

1960 Supplementary Notice No. P.81. L.(W.)D. 1960 From Wednesday 14 to Saturday 24 December (inclusive) 70 pages

Additional Signal Box Opening. 1960 saw the number of 'boxes on extended hours increase to 23 with Botley, Holton Heath and Milborne Port supplementing the list.

Additional Shunting Engines

In addition to locations where additional locomotives were provided in 1958, in 1960 such engines were also rostered at Andover Junction, Battersea Yard, Fareham, Kew Bridge South and Winchester City.

Special Trains

Provision of a standby train, Motorman and Guard between 11.0am and 4.0pm at Waterloo, was not continued.

1960, however, saw resumption of use of Battersea Yard for van trains which hosted the following additional trains: 5.40am (EWD) to Woking, 5.49am (Su) to Bournemouth Central, 2.11pm (EWD) to Woking where attached to 3.12pm Waterloo-Weymouth, 6.11(Su) to Weymouth, 7.42pm (EWD) to Woking and 9.12pm (Su) Woking all via Longhedge Junction, Clapham Junction and East Putney, together with a 2.10pm (Su) to Clapham Yard via Longhedge Junction. Battersea Yard was serviced for empty vans by four trains daily from Nine Elms Yard via Clapham Junction (Kensington Sidings) where reversal took place, plus on Wednesday 14 December, a 4.15am ex-Feltham Yard via Hounslow and Clapham Yard with 38 vanfits and 2 brakes. Battersea Yard returning spare brakes by the 1.12pm (freight) Stewarts Lane to Nine Elms.

Another example of the same; again this is Templecombe where we see No. 41296 leading the 3.35p.m. Templecombe to Blandford Forum service with No. 41242 propelling. The train has just left the platform and is making its way to Templecombe Junction.

A completely new innovation this year was the use of a limited number of loco hauled passenger carrying vehicles on a group of services. Stock used was a complete 3 set, BCK and 2 SKs, 2 BSKs, BCK and 2 SKs. Based at Teddington, this stock worked empty to Waterloo via Twickenham, Waterloo-Richmond via Teddington and Twickenham loaded parcels mostly empty then to Waterloo for further services. There were occasional forays as far as Reading South. An instruction in the P notice stated it was essential formations of these trains were maintained, especially in respect of brake and specially provided passenger vehicles. The reason for use of this stock is unknown although, more likely, knowledge of the reason has been lost in the mists of time.

Two long distance inter-regional van trains were introduced this year: 9.30pm Manchester (Mayfield)-Redhill (daily) via Reading New Junction and Guildford and 11.50pm (not Sundays) Preston-Redhill also via Reading New Junction and Guildford with no similar workings in the opposite direction. A shorter distance new service this year, albeit only on Sunday 18, was an 11.40am Westbury-Weymouth via Yeovil Pen Mill.

No space reserved on the 6.0pm Padstow-Okehampton for rabbit traffic!

Isle of Wight. No special arrangements in 1960.

1961 Supplementary Notice No. P.81 L.(W.)D. 1960 From Wednesday 13 to Sunday 24 December (inclusive) 72 pages

The title page heading of this notice was Southern Region South Western Division, London (Western) Southampton and Exeter Districts rather than Southern Region London (Western) Southern and Western Districts used hitherto.

Additional Opening of Signal Boxes. Number reduced from 23 in 1960 to 21 in 1961 with amended opening times not required at Coleford Junction and Newton St Cyres, but with Dinton as an additional box. Meanwhile Milborne Port box had been renamed Milborne Port Halt to be in line with reduction of the station to Halt status and consequent station renaming.

Making use of another region's motive power, this is the 3.58p.m. Southampton terminus to Eastleigh empty stock train on 6 September 1958. After positioning the vehicles, No. 2252 will pick up its own train of WR coaches bound for the DNS line and Newbury.

Additional Shunting Engines. Additional power withdrawn at Kew Bridge South, Battersea Yard, Winchester City and Fareham.

Additional Trains. By now special trains were not specifically restricted to operating to and from "domestic" Southern Region stations, but becoming wider spread to and from destinations on other regions as will be seen from the summary below:

2.30am MX Guildford-Reading Old Junction. Traffic for widespread areas of the country.

4.30am EWD Salisbury-Bristol Temple Meads

5.0am MX Didcot-Basingstoke

7.40am MX Reading Old Junction-Oxford Rewley Road. Traffic for Western Region and Great Eastern via Oxford.

8.0am EWD Westbury-Salisbury

8.45am MX Didcot-Reading Old Junction via Old Bank with traffic for Southern Region via Redhill

10.05am MX Reading Old Junction-LMR (no exact destination given). Traffic for LMR, ScR and Great Northern.

12.0Noon (17 December only) Bristol Temple Meads-Salisbury

12.15pm (17 December only) Westbury-Weymouth

12.20pm EWD Bristol-Salisbury

6.40pm (17th only) Millbrook-Reading Old Junction

7.12pm (EWD) Margate-Reading Old Junction via Redhill and Guildford

9.15pm (EWD) Bristol Temple Meads-Salisbury

9.25pm (EWD) Millbrook-Market Drayton via Southcote Junction

9.30pm (EWD) Manchester Central Goods-Canterbury West via Reading New Junction and Guildford

11.5pm (EWD) Liverpool Exchange-Canterbury West via Reading New Junction and Guildford

11.23pm (EWD) Brighton-Reading Old Junction via Redhill and Guildford. Neither the 9.30pm Manchester Mayfield-Redhill or 11.30pm Preston-Redhill via Guildford which operated in 1960 ran in 1961.

I think the references above to Oxford (Newley Road) related to Oxford (Rewley Road). NB: 17 December referred to above was a Sunday. Those trains from Waterloo in 1960 which were formed of empties from Teddington and had loco hauled passenger carrying vehicles in their formation were not shown to include such vehicles in 1961. Nevertheless, the P notice still included the cautionary note this year with regard to correct formations being maintained especially with regard to passenger carrying vehicles.

Two individual van movements are interesting. First a van fit conveying Alresford traffic was worked from Eastleigh to Alresford Saturdays excepted on the 12.12pm (Freight) Eastleigh-Alresford. Secondly the Fawley branch was not left out despite its meagre passenger service. A van of parcels, etc. for the branch stations was worked Saturdays excepted from Southampton Terminus to Eastleigh on the 11.8am van train from the former station, and attached at Eastleigh to the 3.0pm passenger thence to Fawley.

Only limited mail and parcels traffic was routed by the DNS line, old habits dying hard, with most inter-regional parcels routed via Basingstoke or Salisbury instead. Consequently there was rarely an excess of parcels vans added to DNS line trains – although horse-boxes were more frequent. Here at Newbury, No. 6302 has arrived from Eastleigh bound for Didcot.

Electric Parcels

The number of such trains increased this year, all formed of 4-SUB units as follows:

10.48amEWD Waterloo-Waterloo via Hounslow and Richmond headcode

11.48amEWD Waterloo-Reading (Southern) non-stop Waterloo to Feltham via Twickenham headcode J

5.48pm (Su) and 9.48pm (EWD) Waterloo-Reading (Southern) via Hounslow headcode T. From Waterloo at 2.14pm (EWD) to Twickenham via Kingston, 3.10pm (Su) and 7.12pm (EWD), to Richmond via Kingston all headcode A.

2.34pm EWD Reading (Southern)-Twickenham

1962 Supplementary Notice No. P.88 L.(Ws)D. 1962 From Thursday 13 to Monday 24 December (inclusive) 76 pages

Additional

Opening of Signal Boxes. It is easier to reissue the summary of boxes involved rather than quote an addendum list. Boxes affected were Alderbury Junction, Blackwater – which was open continuously from 13 until 6.0am 23 December, Bookham, Bow (Devon), Branksome, Cobham, Clandon, Dinton, Holton Heath, Horsley, London Road (Guildford), Lyndhurst Road, Milborne Port Halt, New Milton, North Tawton, Oatlands – open continuously from 13 until 6.0am 24 December, Porton, Sampford Courtenay, Semley, Stoneham, Teddington and Wootton.

Special Instruction. Issued in 1962 to the effect that ALL freight vehicles utilised for Parcel and Mail traffic had to be marked XP

Specific Instructions. An unusual schedule for a road vehicle (on hire to the British Transport Commission) was provided daily to convey Parcels Post traffic making several trips between 3.0pm and 1.30am serving Woking GPO, Godalming GPO, returning to Woking GPO and Guildford station.

There was no change to the additional shunting engines list or Channel Islands sailings summary.

Additional Trains

Little change to the previous year but a few revisions to the inter-regional list of 1961. Last year's summary was virtually unchanged for 1962 but with the more major revisions which were: 7.40amEWD Reading Old Junction-Oxford (Newley Rd) (*sic* – should be Rewley Rd) (the old LNWR/LMS station), started 7.15am and terminated at Scours Lane.

8.45amMX Didcot-Reading Old Junction additional.

10.05am MX Reading Old Junction-LMR destination shown as Crewe (Gresty Lane). 8.30pm (Su) Millbrook-Southampton Old Docks where traffic was attached to 11.0pm SU(Freight) Southampton Old Docks-Crewe.

9.25pm (EWD) Millbrook-Market Drayton destination changed to Rhyl.

The routing of one additional van train, 5.2pmEWD Alton-Woking, to me seemed to jump off the page of the P notice. Normal routing would have been via Ash Vale joining the Bournemouth main line at Pirbright Junction. This year, however, it was routed from Ash Vale to Camberley where the engine ran round and proceeded to Woking via Frimley Junction and over the little used Sturt Lane Spur to Sturt Lane Junction on the Bournemouth main line. In the 1961-62 winter timetable there were but three trains over this spur, all Saturdays excepted in both directions spread over both peak periods.

Electric Parcels Trains

The additional trains shown to run in 1961 also ran in 1962, the only difference being that use of letter headcodes had been discontinued and replaced by numerical codes.

Finally for 1962, it was fortunate that the operational period of this notice had terminated on Christmas Eve. As only two days later – on Boxing Day – the first snowfall of that severe winter struck the south of the country with snow laying for approximately 6-8 weeks causing inevitable general havoc to railway operation.

1963 Supplementary Notice No. P17, 1963. From Monday 9 to Tuesday 24 December (inclusive) 85 pages

I suspect that in so far as Southern Region aficionados are concerned this year was the nadir of the rot setting in with transfer on New Year's Day, of all Southern Region lines west of Salisbury, to the Western Region. In the opposite direction that part of the former Wilts, Somerset and Weymouth line between Castle Cary and Dorchester West was transferred 'back home' to the Western Region. Perhaps less prominent to the travelling public (but very prominent to us who worked in them!) was closure at the end of September of the District Traffic Managers' offices at Woking and Southampton, being amalgamated into the fully functional South Western Divisional Line Manager's organisation with an office at Wimbledon. Consequently the title page of the Christmas P notice was simply headed British Railways Southern Region South Western Division. For 1963 only however, this notice included details of arrangements for Western Region – Plymouth Division former Southern Region Lines.

Additional Opening of Signal Boxes

To the boxes listed for 1962 add Bentley and delete Bow (Devon), Sampford Courtenay and Teddington.

Additional Shunting Engines

Delete Teddington.

The MSWJ route was another cross-country line where parcels and mails were limited although Southern engines were certainly responsible for the few remaining through workings in later years. U No. 31793 at Cheltenham St James in charge of the 1.52pm Cheltenham St James to Southampton Terminus working on 7 November 1959.

Empty Van Trains. More significant writing on the wall in 1963 in that use of Teddington was discontinued for use of berthing empty van trains from various stations, to form onward empties to Waterloo via Twickenham limited to 11 bogies. This work being transferred to Clapham Yard.

With DEMUs taking over the sparse Fawley branch passenger services, the parcels van for Fawley had to transfer to a freight service. The Southampton Terminus Station Master had to arrange for it to be tripped from Southampton Terminus to Northam Yard for attaching next to the engine working the 6.25am (Freight) Eastleigh-Fawley departing Northam Yard at 10.0am.

At least five individual van workings were listed for Somerset and Dorset line services including one on the celebrated 2.40am Bath Green Park-Bournemouth West mail.

1964 Supplementary Notice No. P.91, 1964. From Wednesday 9 until Friday 25 December the word "(inclusive)" not being used after closing date. 80 pages and 24 hour clock adopted.

Additional Opening of Signal Boxes. The detailed list of boxes involved was deleted, no doubt heralding the opening of panel boxes and subsequent closing of mechanical boxes which was beginning to gain momentum. Instead, a general instruction was included worded, "Signal boxes to be open where necessary for the passing of trains shown in this notice. Station Masters to give particular attention to this matter".

Superseded from front line duties by age and the more modern Bulleid and Standard types, No. 30768 *Sir Balin* passes through Salisbury with the 3.00am Brighton-Salisbury (Fisherton yard) freight on 15 July 1961.

Additional Shunting Engines

The complete list of locations was as follows: Aldershot, Andover (as Andover Junction had become), Basingstoke, Bournemouth Central, Clapham Yard, Eastleigh, Eastleigh (Up side), Fratton Yard, Guildford, Hounslow, Millbrook, Nine Elms Hay Yard, Portsmouth & Southsea, Reading (Southern), Salisbury, Southampton Central, Southampton Terminus, Walton-on-Thames (not shown as Oatlands Sidings), Waterloo and Woking East End and Up Yard.

Lymington Branch

With DEMUs having superseded steam passenger services on this branch, an additional parcels train operated – 20.25 Lymington Town-Brockenhurst, yet there was no balancing working in the opposite direction.

Bordon Branch

The special instruction regarding mail for Bordon not included for 1964.

Mail Traffic Alfred Road (WR) to Reading (Southern). This long standing instruction, which had an air of mystery as to the location of Alfred Road, was replaced by a similar one for mail traffic to Reading (Southern) from Paddington (Ladbroke). Had the Alfred Road location been renamed?

West of England Line

This, of course, was the first year the Western Region was 'flexing its muscles'. We find that apart from the long established 01.50MX Eastleigh-Yeovil Town passenger and mail train, there was an 18.35(Su)/19.02(EWD) Waterloo-Exeter Central additional parcels, still conveying vans for Plymouth via Tavistock, Padstow, Bude, Torrington (conveying traffic also for Ilfracombe), Exeter Central, Yeovil Town (also conveying traffic for the Somerset and Dorset) and Salisbury. In the up direction a 23.15(SX) Exeter Central-Nine Elms J1 Shed conveying traffic from virtually the same stations as the down train. Its Saturday counterpart was a 20.00 Yeovil Junction-Waterloo which included three empty newspaper vans (not to be loaded) from Yeovil Junction to Clapham Junction, a vanfit from Plymouth to Waterloo which was attached at Clapham Junction off a previous up train plus an assortment of vans already attached at Basingstoke and Woking.

Somerset and Dorset

Not yet closed in 1964 but still three services conveying individual vans. But none on the 02.40 Bath-Bournemouth West although still running.

General van working

Vans for Alresford and Fawley were withdrawn. In the Southampton area Millbrook yard was bring used for far more parcel and mail trains including on Sundays an 18.40 to Reading Old Junction which had in its formation a steam fitted brake van with traffic for Tonbridge and transfer and Ashford (Kent) and transfer. A new service this year, 07.55(Su)/08.05(EWD) Newbury-Reading Old Junction with traffic from West Country stations to Redhill. The 17.02 Alton-Woking did not run via the Sturt Lane Spur this year.

Electric Parcels Trains

This was the first year that specific 4-SUB units 4355 and 4378 were designated to work only on these services as was shown in Electric Carriage Working notices issued by Wimbledon Line Manager's Office. Furthermore they were not under any circumstances to form other passenger services during the operating period of the P notice. There was also an instruction with regard to removing chalk marks, and cushion brushing, before any other EMUs used in parcels trains returned to passenger train working. Waterloo Station Master had to provide two men (sic) to travel on certain electric parcel trains to assist with parcels traffic. In addition a standby (EMUT) [EMU for parcels use] and guard had to be made available at Waterloo between 10.00 and 16.00 daily except Sundays to work additional electric parcels trains as necessary.

Road Vehicle Working Woking/Guildford/Godalming

A road vehicle on hire to the B.R.B. was provided daily except Sundays to convey parcel post traffic from Woking and Godalming Post Offices to Guildford station. Detailed timings were not shown at intermediate loading/unloading points, only arrival times at Woking Drill Hall and Godalming Post Office.

1965 Supplementary Notice No. P.108, 1965. From Thursday 9 until Saturday 25 December 78 pages

Additional opening of signal boxes

As in 1964 left to Area Managers/Station Masters as necessary, but this year note Area Managers also included.

Still at Salisbury, S15 No. 30827 arrives with the stopping 10.37am Exeter Central to Salisbury service.

Additional Shunting Engines

Andover, Eastleigh up Side and Reading (Southern) deleted but Twickenham and Weymouth added.

Special Instructions

Use of 4-SUBs 4355 and 4378 not specifically highlighted, being replaced by a general term instruction, "It is essential that the two electric suburban units allocated for parcels work only as instructed."

Van Services. Reading (Southern) closed on 6 September 1965 and all van activity hitherto carried out there transferred to Reading General or routed on inter-regional services to such destinations as Scours Lane. As a consequence of this closure the very long standing instruction regarding mail from Alfred Road (WR) to Reading General with traffic for Reading (Southern) disappeared.

New services this year were:

20.08(EWD) Hastings-Scours Lane via Redhill and Guildford,

21.05(EWD) Sidcup-Scours Lane via Redhill and Guildford,

23.10(EWD) Purley-Scours Lane via Sutton, Epsom and Guildford (reverse),

21.15(EWD) Nottingham Victoria-Canterbury West via Reading and Redhill, and 21.20(EWD) Millbrook-Whitchurch (Salop) via Southcote Junction with mainly vanfits for Eastern, North- East and North-West England going through with detachments at Eastleigh for the West of England, Cardiff and Bristol and at Basingstoke North Yard for several widely scattered Southern Region destinations.

The Somerset and Dorset, not surprisingly so close to closure, had no individual through vans.

1966 Supplementary Notice No. P.115, 1966. From Sunday 11 until Sunday 25 December 84 pages

Additional opening hours of signal boxes again left to Area/Station Managers' discretion. Note Station Masters now re-designated Station Managers.

Southampton Terminus. This station closed on 5 September 1966 so not requiring an additional shunting engine during the Christmas period. Nevertheless it reopened in part to deal with Christmas Mails and Parcels traffic, an unusual procedure once a station had been closed, being served by the following special van trains: 00.15 and 05.56 ex-Southampton Central, 01.00

Finally, the Western influence at Salisbury, where engines were usually changed on the inter-regional workings. This is 'Castle' No. 5087 *Tintern Abbey* in charge of the 2.45pm Portsmouth & Southsea to Bristol Temple Meads train.

Eastleigh-Northam Yard extended to Southampton Terminus, 03.45am ex- Southampton Eastern Docks which really was nothing more than a shunt movement from one side of Canute Road to the other, this thoroughfare separating the two establishments, 04.15, 07.40, 15.10, 17.15, 20.30 and 23.15 ex-Northam Yard, 07.52 ex-Eastleigh and the 21.40 Eastleigh-Southampton Central diverted to Southampton Terminus. It is difficult to visualise that Northam Yard is now the site of the Siemens EMU depot. From this list it will be deduced that only inwards traffic was dealt with at this station and presumably, all outwards traffic at Southampton Central. So how were the unloaded vans dispersed? By two empty van trains to Bevois Park (now Southampton Up Yard) at 07.10 and 09.00 plus a longer distance service at 22.30 to Clapham Junction.

Special Van Trains

Interesting to note the 15.00(Su) Waterloo-Bournemouth Central and 15.44(EWD) Waterloo-Weymouth conveyed – if required – empty milk tanks from Vauxhall to Bailey Gate over the remaining rump of the Somerset and Dorset via Poole. But the P notice did not make it clear how the empty milk tanks were worked from Vauxhall to Waterloo. The following is a summary of inter-regional trains which demonstrate the growing practice of running more trains crossing inter-regional borders rather than exchanging vans from region to region at 'border' stations, plus the fact that rationalisation of facilities was becoming rife. In so far as this article is concerned inter-regional services include those on the former Southern west of England line proceeding beyond Salisbury and, following closure of Reading (Southern), were dealt with at Reading General or Scours Lane:

01.45(EWD), 03.15(EWD) and 04.05(EWD) Guildford-Scours Lane

03.15(EWD) Reading General-Redhill

04.15(EWD) Salisbury-Exeter Central

04.30 (EWD) Stratford-Redhill via Kensington Olympia, Clapham Junction, Woking and Guildford 04.45 (Su) Reading General-Redhill 08.08(EWD) Hinksey Up Yard-Redhill via Reading General 09.15(Daily) Reading General-Basingstoke West Yard

Double heading was never as common on the Southern as it was elsewhere but here we see two members of the U class, Nos. 31623 and 31626, passing St Denys on the 10.43am Southampton terminus to Eastleigh special ECS working, Richard recorded the time at 11.10a.m on a dull 8 July 1961. Notice the make-up of the train; a mixture of passenger and van stock.

09.40(EWD) Guildford-Cambridge via Woking, East Putney, Clapham and Latchmere junctions 10.50(Su)/ 13.00(Su)/17.20(EWD) Hinksey Up Sidings-Redhill via Reading General and Guildford 15.30(EWD) Reading General-Basingstoke West Yard

18.40(Su) Millbrook-Reading General

19.27 (EWD) Reading General-Waterloo via Twickenham. Two porters were required to travel with this train as far as Feltham to assist with parcels traffic.

21.28(EWD)/21.35(Su) Bristol Temple Meads-Salisbury

22.05(EWD) Millbrook-Whitchurch (Salop) via Southcote Junction

23.15(EWD) Twickenham-Scours Lane via Reading General

23.30 (EWD & Su) Exeter Central-Waterloo

Oatlands sidings was still used for formation and remarshalling of some up trains but not to the extent of more recent years; South Lambeth was not used in 1966. Number of individual van movements vastly reduced down to 23 items of which only 1 related to a movement west of Salisbury.

1969 Supplementary Notice No. P.101, 1969 operative Monday 8 until Thursday 25 December 87 pages

This is the final year for which I have a Christmas Mails and Parcels Traffic notice and, of course, it was a different era to the 1952 notice. Steam had gone and the Bournemouth electrification had been inaugurated in July 1967. With it came a completely recast timetable and the same situation applied for van trains, the only difference being that with the exception of inter-regional trains there were no passenger services to which the odd van or two could be attached. In the 1969 P notice gone were the lists of additional shunting locomotives and amended opening hours of signal boxes, but Area/Station Managers were still reminded it was their responsibility to ensure boxes were open for the passing of trains shown in the notice, the full programme of Panel Box introduction on the Division still had to be completed. The table of Channel Islands sailings from Weymouth and Southampton over the Christmas period still found a place in the notice, full concentration of all this traffic on Weymouth was yet to come. Station Managers still had to report in writing to the Divisional Manager – not later than 9 January 1970 – pointing out any alterations calculated to improve future working. Furthermore they had to arrange for a record to be made of the quantity of traffic received and despatched by each service.

So I think for this notice special trains will be summarised over different routes, just noting any unusual or distinctive features which stand out. Again empty trains will not be listed or any regular timetabled trains which are cancelled or revised in any way. Motive power will be assumed to be diesel locomotive (DL) hauled with no special note being made of this. Electro diesel (EDL) locomotives were not shown to haul any van train but there are a few examples of diesel shunting locomotives being used, and this will be noted as being shown as DSL. With electrification more electric multiple units were utilised and this will be noted by being shown as EMU. Dates of special train operation remain variable and space does not permit listing those. Trains running Sundays only will be so indicated as Su, otherwise trains run each weekday unless shown.

Oatlands sidings had ceased to be used for shunting and train formations but South Lambeth was back. A new instruction was that the length of down parcels trains arriving at Bournemouth (as Bournemouth Central had become) must not exceed =10 bogies. Also what was described as a quick method of assessing the length of a train was to count the vehicles thus:

GUV, BG, Siphon or other bogie vehicle, 3 units PMV, SPV, BY, CCT, Conflat D and all six-wheeled vehicles, 1½ units Vanfits, 1 unit.

Total the units, divide by 3 and round off to the next higher whole number. This gives the approximate length of the train in bogies. I think it can well be imagined many Guards would have struggled calculating this formula on a dark and damp winter's night in December with the only lighting being a Bardic hand lamp or even one of the old paraffin fuelled flame hand lamps, perhaps rather poor yard lighting and also no calculator to assist with the calculation! Brainwork required, I think.

The Woking-Godalming road vehicle was still hired although in 1969 it was on hire to the GPO and not the BRB.

It will be observed that Shalford was used quite extensively but pass through the station today and one would wonder where on earth the sidings used to be. On the West of England line, there was only one special west of Salisbury.

On the Isle of Wight with the decimation of the Island railway system and electrification of the remaining Ryde Pier Head-Shanklin stub, traffic was conveyed by what was described as "trunk road motor services" by the 03.05 Portsmouth-Fishbourne car ferry which "must leave on time". It is to be hoped that this instruction was relayed to the clerk of the weather, who co-operated by banning thick fog or gales during the pre-Christmas period so that boats were not delayed crossing Spithead!

So to the train summary:

Bournemouth Main Line

00.25 Basingstoke-South Lambeth via East Putney and Longhedge Junction

02.40 Basingstoke-Waterloo via Chertsey and Hounslow

02.45 Eastleigh-Southampton Eastern Docks

04.20 South Lambeth-Basingstoke via Longhedge Junction, Hounslow and Chertsey

12.00 Didcot Up Yard-Bournemouth extended to Weymouth on Sundays

18.30(Su) Southampton Western Docks-Reading General via Basingstoke

'Special Empties' passing St Denys on 8 October 1962. No. 73020 working what was the 9.50a.m. Bournemouth West to Clapham Junction service.

18.40 South Lambeth-Northam Yard but terminated at Eastleigh Saturdays and Sundays, via Longhedge and Clapham Junctions and Hounslow

18.43 Bournemouth-Waterloo EMU

19.55 Weymouth-South Lambeth via East Putney, Clapham and Longhedge junctions

21.20 Waterloo-Weymouth

21.50 Weymouth-Salisbury via Eastleigh

22.45 Portsmouth & Southsea-Basingstoke via Eastleigh

23.10 Bournemouth-Weymouth

23.48 Woking-Waterloo EMU

Portsmouth Direct Line

00.01 Portsmouth & Southsea-South Lambeth via Guildford, East Putney and Longhedge Junction 00.30 Guildford-Waterloo via Woking EMU

01.15 Woking-Portsmouth & Southsea

05.58 Channelsea-Guildford via Kensington (Olympia), Clapham Junction, Twickenham, Chertsey and Woking

06.15(Su) Woking-Guildford

10.30 Guildford-Woking

11.16 Woking East End-Portsmouth & Southsea

11.39 Portsmouth & Southsea-Haslemere EMU

Micheldever sidings was one of the locations where stock might be stored pending peaks in traffic but also of course awaiting works attention. The sheds in the distance were erected in WW2 and comically known as 'Woolworths'; meaning they were a place where it was jokingly said almost everything for the military might be obtained in whatever colour and whatever size. *S/Way collection*

12.50 Haslemere-Havant EMU

13.20 Waterloo-Portsmouth & Southsea

15.35 Guildford-Woking

19.00 (Su) Guildford-Woking

22.20 (Su) Woking-Portsmouth & Southsea

22.30 Portsmouth & Southsea-Guildford

23.45 Guildford-Woking

Former West of England Line

02.55 Basingstoke-Salisbury

04.30 (05.00Su) Salisbury-Yeovil Junction

21.45MO Salisbury-Basingstoke

22.45 Salisbury-Basingstoke

Suburban Services

All EMU:

10.12, 14.12 and 22.12 Guildford-Sutton

10.18 Waterloo-Leatherhead

11.05, 15.05 and 23.05 Sutton-Effingham Junction

11.40 and 14.10 Waterloo-Shepperton via Kingston

11.42 Guildford-Surbiton via Cobham 12.44 and 15.14 Shepperton-Waterloo via Kingston

15.30(Su) Waterloo-Richmond via Kingston

18.00 (Su) Waterloo-Surbiton via Twickenham, Ascot, Aldershot (reverse) and Woking

19.27 Hampton Court-Waterloo

On certain of the above mentioned trains the Area Manager, Waterloo, had to provide two men to travel on them to assist with parcels traffic. Also a standby EMUT driver and guard had to be available at Waterloo from 10.00 to 16.00 daily except Sundays to work additional electric parcels trains as necessary.

Non-EMU

01.20 Clapham Yard-South Lambeth via Longhedge Junction

03.20MO Clapham Yard-Waterloo

03.50MO Clapham Junction-South Lambeth via Longhedge Junction

Woking-Alton

02.00 Woking-Alton

10.50 Guildford-Surbiton via Farnham (reverse) EMU

13.16 Woking-Alton

21.20(Su) Woking-Alton

22.30 Aldershot-Guildford

23.43 Aldershot-Waterloo EMU

Reading-Basingstoke

03.07(Su) Reading General-Basingstoke

03.30(Su) Didcot-Basingstoke

06.00 Basingstoke Up Yard-Reading General

Waterloo-Reading and Windsor Lines

00.30 Twickenham-Rugby via Richmond and Latchmere Junction

04.15 Waterloo-Clapham Junction via Kingston and Twickenham

11.30 & 12.30 Waterloo-Camberley via Hounslow EMU

14.32 Clapham Yard-Nottingham via Barnes and Kew East Junction

20.30 Waterloo-Staines via Hounslow and Twickenham (reverse) EMU

21.30 Waterloo-Camberley via Hounslow EMU

21.54 Guildford-Richmond via Farnham (reverse) and Camberley EMU

21.55 Wokingham-Waterloo via Twickenham

Redhill – Reading General

00.05 Brighton-Shalford via Redhill

00.45 Guildford-Shalford DSL

02.00 Guildford-Shalford

05.00 Shalford-Guildford

05.45 Shalford-Crewe via Reading General

06.40 Shalford-Oxford via Reading General

06.45(Su) Reading General-Redhill

08.45 Shalford-York via Reading General

09.25 Shalford-Cambridge via Woking, Twickenham, Clapham and Latchmere junctions

13.15 & 15.35 Didcot-Redhill via Guildford

20.07 Hastings-Shalford via Redhill

20.10 Margate-Shalford via Redhill

21.49 Dartford-Shalford via Redhill

23.57 East Croydon-Shalford via Redhill

Westbury-Salisbury-Portsmouth

02.30 Portsmouth & Southsea-Eastleigh

02.55 Salisbury-Portsmouth & Southsea via Eastleigh and Botley or Eastleigh, Northam Yard (reverse) and Netley

05.05(Su) Portsmouth & Southsea-Eastleigh

05.50 Salisbury-Bristol Temple Meads

14.10 Bristol West Depot-Southampton (as Southampton Central had become) via Eastleigh

20.28 Southampton-Bristol Temple Meads via Redbridge and Romsey

21.10 Bristol Temple Meads-Salisbury

Portsmouth-Brighton (West Coast Line)

04.55 Portsmouth & Southsea-Brighton

20.24 Chichester-Portsmouth & Southsea

21.33 Portsmouth & Southsea-Brighton via Bognor Regis (reverse). Train formation includes vanfit into which Littlehampton traffic was loaded. From P notice unable to establish whether train also ran into and out of Littlehampton, or whether Littlehampton traffic together with that for Arundel and Horsham went into Littlehampton or was transferred at – probably – Barnham.

22.27 Brighton-Portsmouth and Southsea.

Another 'King Arthur', this time No. 30743 *Lyonnesse,* reversed in to the up platform at Dorchester South en-route from Weymouth to Bournemouth. *S/Way collection*

A Standard Class 4 seemingly reversing into the Baltic siding at Winchester with parcels vans. *S/Way collection*

The notice concluded with the usual summary of timetabled services conveying vehicles in addition to their usual formations plus a new feature not come across previously, a summary of normal scheduled vans withdrawn together with those "reserviced" (a new term replacing the more well known description "revised") to alternative services!

One further interesting instruction related to Kent parcel mails. GPO parcel mail for Kent destinations had to be routed via South Lambeth for GPO transfer to London Bridge. Vans had not to be despatched to London Bridge or Canterbury and other South Eastern Division stations, unless there was sufficient traffic to one destination to justify direct loading.

So conveyance of mail traffic has largely but not totally disappeared. I say not totally disappeared because whilst quickly glancing through 'Freightmaster No.96', January-March 2020 by Mark Rawlinson and published by Freightmaster Publishing, I came across a handful of mail trains -Mondays-Fridays formed of Class 325 EMUs; 16.05 Willesden PRDC-Shieldmuir, 19.25 Warrington RMT-Willesden PRDC and on the East Coast Main Line, 21.43 Low Fell-RMT-Willesden PRDC and 22.45 Willesden PRDC-Low Fell RMT. But loading and unloading mail at ordinary station platforms has probably totally disappeared, transferred to huge lorries chugging along the Motorway network or, maybe, taking to the air. And whilst 'Beechingisation' was taking place on the railways, similar action was doubtless proceeding in the GPO/Royal Mail organisation such as cutting out smaller sorting offices, etc.

The absence of overnight trains which conveyed both passengers and mail, often following routes not traversed by daytime through services, leaves large gaps in services. On Sunday nights/Monday mornings these were well frequented by National Servicemen (such as myself) returning to camp from weekend leave. As for railway enthusiasts wanting to do some 'route bashing', it is no longer possible to join the train which started from York at 9.48pm, remaining on it overnight until journey's end the following morning at Swansea Victoria at 8.4am having passed through – amongst other places – Leeds City, Huddersfield, Stalybridge, Crewe, Shrewsbury and the Central Wales line. In mid-Summer on a fine morning it must have been a very scenic and exhilarating ride over the latter line.

Preparation of this article took far longer than anticipated and a gargantuan task, but I hope the end result does give an insight into the complicated and often involved task of moving and delivering the nation's Christmas mail and parcels often utilising lines and stations which have now long since been obliterated from the railway map. I'm going to stick my head out and say it could not be done today in a similar manner.

So, Christmas mails and parcels *requiescant*.

Acknowledgments

Atlas of Railway Station Closures. Crecy Publishing Ltd 2018

Atlas of the Southern Railway. R. Harman and G. Nichols. Ian Allan Publishing Ltd 2016

Signal Box Register. Signalling Record Society

1963 Bradshaw's Guide. January 1948

Various Southern Region public timetables.

Various British Railways Southern Region South Western Division Special Traffic Notices and WTTs

My Personal Memory!

More parcels workings, this time having just left Winchester northbound. Alongside is the regular Winchester shunter/pilot, a member of the B4 class. The view is taken from the Andover Road bridge. *S/Way collection*

Mail van S4960, the location identified by the buildings in the background, meaning it has to be Southampton.

Abbreviations

AM	Area Manager
BRB	British Railways Board
CWN	Carriage Working Notices
DL	Diesel Locomotive
DSL	Diesel Shunting Locomotive
ECS	Empty Coaching Stock
EDL	Electro Diesel Locomotive
EMU	Electric Multiple Unit
EMUT	Electric Multiple Unit Trained
EWD	Every Weekday
GPO	General Post Office
LMR	London Midland Region
L&SWR	London & South Western Railway
MO	Mondays Only
MPD	Motive Power Depot
MX	Mondays Excepted
P	Notice Special Traffic Printed Notice
POS	Post Office Sorting Vehicle
POT	Post Office Tender Vehicle
Q	Service Runs If Required
SM	Station Master (became Station Manager)
SN	Stencil Special Traffic Notice
SR	Southern Region
ST	Special Traffic
Su	Sundays Only
TPO	Travelling Post Office
WR	Western Region
WTT	Working Time Table

A favourite location of many (your Editor included). Ventnor West, undated, and 'Terrier' No. W11 soon to set off for the return to Merstone Junction.

More on the 'PEP' Sets

Les Price

Back in Issue 22 (April 2013) an article was presented on the three PEP units (one 2-car and two 4-car) destined to have a short life on the Southern Region.

Since that time some limited new information and images have come to light including this comment from the archives of John Click, "What is probably not generally known is when the Locomotive Drawing Office did the first diagram, for a double decker set, it was shown as a five-car articulated effort. When scrapped, but not life-expired on their books, an accountant's fluke was used to justify building the prototype PEP trains, which have sired the ever-proliferating new generation of suburban sets. But they all have far fewer seats and cost (in real terms) multiples of even this, the most expensive of all Bulleid's otherwise standardised and very cost-effective electric stock."

Above: **We start at Waterloo, and the solitary 2-car set No. 2001. The No. 30 route number indicates a Waterloo – Hampton Court service.** *Graham Smith courtesy Richard Sissons*

Opposite top: **At destination, No. 2001 is in as built aluminium livery at Hampton Court.** *Graham Smith courtesy Richard Sissons*

Bottom: **No detail as to which set, 2 or 4 car but the interior of an almost complete Pep unit at Derby.** *Graham Smith courtesy Richard Sissons*

2001
2001
30

The second of the four car units, brand new at Derby. The APT set will be noted alongside. *Graham Smith courtesy Richard Sissons*

At Waterloo in standard BR Blue. The continuation of the yellow around the front allied to the low height creates a bulbous appearance especially when compared with the 4-SUB set alongside. *Douglas Twiball/Transport Treasury*

SET 50

Second Generation EMU prototype - 2car.

D.M.O. WIMBLEDON — SPECIAL NOTICE NO. 274 S.W.D. — 6TH APRIL, 1973.

MONDAY 9TH APRIL

(1) CREW TRAINING WITH CLASS 31 LOCO

Headcode/Train No.	5Z65
SALISBURY YARD	10 00 A
Tunnel Jn.	10/04
Andover	10/29
Worting Jn.	10/55 SL
Basingstoke	11/00
BARTON MILL C.S.	11 03

Headcode/Train No.	5Z65
BARTON MILL C.S.	11 22 A
Basingstoke	11/26 FL
Worting Jn.	11/30
Andover	11/55
Tunnel Jn.	12/20
Salisbury	12c26
SALISBURY YARD	12 29

A - Formed DL, 3 coaches, 15 empty vanfits.

TUESDAY 10TH TO THURSDAY 12TH APRIL

(2) HEATING TESTS WITH 2 PEP 2001 (C.M. & E.E. A/C)

HEADCODE/TRAIN NO.	WThO 21/5Z61	WThO‡ 21/5Z61	21/5Z61	21/5Z61	21/5Z61	21/5Z61	21/5Z61
CLAPHAM JUNCTION		10†40SL	11†40SL	12†40SL	13†40SL	14†40SL	15†40SL
Wandsworth Town		10 42	11 42	12 42	13 42	14 42	15 42
Pt. Pleasant Jn.		10/44	11/44	12/44	13/44	14/44	15/44
East Putney		10/46	11/46	12/46	13/46	14/46	15/46
Southfields		10 48½	11 48½	12 48½	13 48½	14 48½	15 48½
Wimbledon Park		10 50½	11 50½	12 50½	13 50½	14 50½	15 50½
Wimbledon		10/54SL	11/54SL	12/54SL	13/54SL	14/54SL	15/54SL
Raynes Park		10 57	11 57	12 57	13 57	14 57	15 57
New Malden		11 00	12 00	13 00	14 00	15 00	16 00
Norbiton		11 03	12 03	13 03	14 03	15 03	16 03
Kingston		11 05	12 05	13 05	14 05	15 05	16 05
Teddington		11 08½	12 08½	13 08½	14 08½	15 08½	16 08½
Strawberry Hill Depot	10†08						16†18
Strawberry Hill	10/11	11/11	12/11	13/11	14/11	15/11	
Twickenham	10 13½FL	11 13½FL	12 13½FL	13 13½FL	14 13½FL	15 13½FL	
St. Margarets	10 15½	11 15½	12 15½	13 15½	14 15½	15 15½	
Richmond	10 18	11 18	12 18	13 18	14 18	15 18	
North Sheen	10 20½	11 20½	12 20½	13 20½	14 20½	15 20½	
Mortlake	10 22½	11 22½	12 22½	13 22½	14 22½	15 22½	
Barnes	10 25½SL	11 25½SL	12 25½SL	13 25½SL	14 25½SL	15 25½SL	
Putney	10 28½	11 28½	12 28½	13 28½	14 28½	15 28½	
Wandsworth Town	10 31½	11 31½	12 31½	13 31½	14 31½	15 31½	
CLAPHAM JUNCTION	10†33½	11†33½	12†33½	13†33½	14†33½	15†33½	

STATIONS TO ENSURE THAT NO PASSENGERS JOIN THESE TRAINS.

‡TO: Start Wimbledon Park Sdgs. 10†49, Wimbledon 10/54 SL, thence as in column 2 for WThO

TRAIN ALTERATIONS

09 04 Guildford to Waterloo (AS) - Run FL from Barnes
(REPEAT EACH HOUR UNTIL 14 04 Guildford to Waterloo).
11 04 Waterloo (W) to Camberley - Depart Kingston 12 10, run 6 mins. later to Twickenham. 5 mins later to Feltham and 4 mins. later to Virginia Water.

SPECIAL WORKING INSTRUCTIONS

The above trains must NOT:
(1) Exceed a speed of 20 m.p.h. through New Malden and Hampton Wick stations.
(2) Run via the Up Slow Line Twickenham to St. Margarets.

SPECIAL NOTICE NO. 274 S.W.D.
SHEET NO. 1 (CONTINUED)

Finally, details of a test run with set No. 2001 from Clapham Junction to Strawberry Hill and return on 6 April 1973. *Les Price collection*

Mr Jacomb-Hood and the Premium System of Track Inspection

From 'The Railway Gazette', 13 March 1914

The late Mr Jacomb-Hood was the first engineer to apply, with suitable modifications to English practice, the American premium system of track inspection. This praiseworthy novelty he introduced in 1904, and it continued to be held annually for several years. Various causes contributed towards its enforced suspension of late, but only a few weeks ago the present writer received a letter from the deceased gentleman stating how eagerly and confidently he was looking forward to its early restoration. We believe that nothing so thorough and scientific of the kind has ever been tried in this country outside the London & SouthWestern Railway. The present writer, who enjoyed the friendship of Mr Jacomb-Hood, was privileged to accompany him on these inspections, of which some account may now be given.

Mr J. W. Jacomb-Hood M.Inst C.E. John Wykeham Jacomb-Hood was born in 1859 and educated at Tonbridge School and at the Crystal Palace School of Engineering. He became a pupil to the then chief engineer to the London & SouthWestern Railway Company in 1875. From 1878 to 1887 he served in the capacity of assistant engineer to the Company, carrying out the construction of various new works. For the next eight years he was District Engineer in charge of the permanent way and works in the London district, afterwards being transferred in 1895 to the Western district. In 1901 he became Chief Resident Engineer, a position that he held until his death, which took place suddenly at a meet of the Dulverton Hounds on the 6 March 1914. He was responsible for the carrying out and maintenance of much of the electrical work of the Company, and took great interest in the question of electrification. He was also involved in the reconstruction of Waterloo Station. (Information courtesy Grace's Guide.)

First, as to the purport of the system: it sought to apportion rightly, and to check the expenditure on maintenance and renewal of permanent way, and at the same time to obtain better results for the same, if not less, money. It emphasised the principle that unless the road-bed – the foundations of a railway – be constructed of the soundest material and scientifically maintained, it is useless to expect that the employment of the heaviest and most costly track equipment will produce the desired efficiency and economy. Therefore, in order to get a better road and at less cost, endeavour must be concentrated upon educating up the gangers and those under them. The old idea of regarding this class of workers as mere labourers is exploded. They should be taught to put brains into the road as well as muscle. There is only one way to make the men at the bottom understand that better things are expected of them, viz., by showing them that their work is going to be individually examined and compared every year by the head officials. There is only one way to make them turn out better work than previously, viz., by instilling them with a spirit of emulation and encouraging them with the offer of money and other prizes. This is how Mr Jacomb-Hood's scheme was conducted. The SouthWestern Railway is divided into three districts, each of which is in charge of a district engineer, and subdivided into 36 inspectors' divisions. A divisional inspector takes from 35 to 50 miles of single track. Next come the foremen gangers, whose length of road averages 2 miles on the double track or about 4 miles on the single. Below these overseers come the platelayers or surface men, who work in gangs, and the number of whom in a gang varies according to the density of traffic on the respective gang lengths.

Everybody's responsibility was reduced to a common basis by charging him with the equivalent single line mileage he had to maintain. He had so many running miles under him plus miles of sidings, of which 2 miles were reckoned equal to 1 mile of the former, while he was also credited with another mile of running mile for every 15 sets of points. The Chief Engineer's Road Book was arranged in consecutive order of inspectors' sections as follows:

(1) Geographical beginning and end of section

(2) Subdivision of running lines, i.e., mileage of single, double, triple track, etc.

(3) Total length in single-line miles

(4) Total length of sidings

(5) Number of points

(6) Total equivalent of points in single-line miles.

Next came particulars of the manning, viz

(1) Names of foremen and their rates of pay

(2) Number of men under each foreman and their rates of pay

(3) Total equivalent single-line mileage divided by the total number of men in gang, which produced the ratio of manning per single-line mile.

It will therefore be seen that for arriving at comparisons the unit of expenditure was brought down to the inspector of each section. The track inspection occupied about eight days, spread over a month or six weeks in the spring. The main line could only be examined on Sundays. Examining Committees were formed as follows:

Class A: For condition of rail joints, alignment of track, and general condition of running surface of rails.

Class B: For condition of ballasting.

Class C: General appearance of all works, including hedges, fences, slopes, drains, footpaths, notice boards, quarter-mile posts, etc.

The premium awards consisted of a silver challenge cup and money prize of £2 for the best inspector's section, and a challenge cup for the best foreman's length throughout the line. With the challenge cups went silver medals to keep. In each inspector's section the foreman with the best length was awarded £1 and a bronze medal, while every man under the prize foreman received a bonus of 10s. and a bronze medal. The awards were arrived at in the following manner:

Reported as 'Engineers' Track inspection Train on the summit of Dartmoor'. Perhaps better known in railway language as at Meldon.

A similar combination at Exmouth.

the line was divided into the respective gang's lengths, and so many marks allotted to each foreman under the three different classes by which the work was judged. In Class A the maximum number of marks was 200, in Class B 120, and in Class C 80. But the method of marking made allowance for certain correcting factors.

It is manifestly to the advantage of a railway company to get the work efficiently done by as few men as possible, and it is calculated that a ratio of one man per single-line mile should suffice. Therefore, one mark was allowed for every 1-100th of a man below one man per mile, and one mark was deducted for every 1-100th of a man above that quota. In deference to the feeling among the men that the age of the road also ought to count for something, the average life of the road was assumed to be 17 years, and for each year in excess of 17 five marks were added to the score, and for each year below 17 two marks were deducted; the object of this discrepancy being to encourage men to take pains with stretches of old road. It was hoped eventually to apply other correcting factors in respect of the density, weight, and speeds of the traffic passing over the different sections.

The inspection train was made up of engine, inspection car, resting saloon, refreshment saloon, inspection car. The inspection car at the tail of the train pro temp was alone used for examining, two of these cars being necessary, because the engine pushed, instead of drew, the train up branches. The inspection car was equipped with two tiers of seats, arranged in two pairs. The examiners sat with their backs to the engine, and scrutinised the receding track. The committee for Class A occupied the seats in the front left-hand corner, and the committee for Class B those in the front right-hand corner, while the committee for Class C sat in the back seats, where they could see over the heads of the former. To ensure impartiality, no examiner was connected with the section under examination, but the inspector of each section was in the car while it passed over it. The latter had marked out the various gangs' lengths by means of white-painted crosses at the side of the track, and he stood behind the examiners to answer questions, and to notify the change from one ganger's length to another, at the same time mentioning each of his foremen by name.

On taking up their position the Secretary of the Inspection Committee handed to each member of the three committees their marking cards. The cards for each class were of different colours, and there was a separate card for each ganger's length. These cards furnished details of each gang's length – the age of the road, weight of rails, etc. and at the foot were spaces for the examiners' notes and awards. At the expiration of their turn of duty, which usually lasted about an hour, examiners returned their cards to the Secretary, and their places were taken by others. The work of examination demanded unflagging attention, and it was rather a bilious business gazing at the track receding from one. The speed of the train while inspecting was limited to 20 miles an hour.

Occasionally the examiners for Class A alighted to inspect the wear of rails, adjustment of points, correctness of gauge, and degree of super-elevation of outer rail round a curve. In 1904 the tunnels were lighted up with flares, but it was found that no satisfactory inspection of the permanent way in a tunnel could be effected from the train. So tunnels were afterwards left to the inspectors, but as no man has a stretch of road wholly in tunnel it was possible to judge his work from that portion of it in the open. To the outsider privileged to participate in these inspections they proved a most interesting and instructive experience. No fault or good point seemed to escape the eyes of the examiners, whose bodies were also strained to catch the slightest shock or oscillation.

The inspection cars were four-wheeled vehicles, so that all shocks from the road might be felt by the body. It was curious to note how one foreman's length would differ from that of another. Here you came across a man whose hedges, fences, and cesses were in model repair, but whose ballast held pools of water, and whose rail joints were out of vertical alignment; and there you travelled through another length where the exact reverse was the case. Sometimes you passed over miles of track where everything was in the most perfect order. The results furnished by this system of track inspection are understood to have been of a most gratifying character. The lowering of the unit of expenditure to a point where comparisons between the different inspectors' sections were rendered possible enabled considerable economies being effected, and, at the same time, secured a greatly improved road. There was no lack of evidence that the system introduced a new spirit of efficiency among all ranks and led to keen rivalry as to who should earn the distinction of turning out the best stretches of track. (The article was contributed to the RG by 'H.G.A.')

Interior view of the saloon. The seating is perhaps slightly more spartan than might have been expected.

Dr John L. Farmer, 1913-1960
A Winchester Enthusiast
Courtesy of Di Jeans, Captions and Notes by Mike Vokes

The term 'railways and Vicars' is well known. Perhaps slightly less so is that of 'railways and Doctors' but it is certainly just as applicable. Due to his profession Dr Farmer was well known in the area although by ancestry he hailed from across the Scottish border. His interest in railways seems to have germinated whilst living in Winchester, where he also cultivated the friendship of a number of railwaymen including signalman 'Tinny' Timpson, one of the regular men at Shawford Junction. It was likely through this friendship that he was able to find out in advance details of any unusual workings, and then if time and his professional commitments permitted, he would record the event on film. The pair also contributed a number of articles on local railways to the 'Hampshire Chronicle' under the pseudonym 'T.J.'

We start with an evening goods train passing Shawford Junction northbound. The locomotive (unusually) is an H15 No. 30332, allocated at the time to Salisbury, and is working the Nine Elms duty 68. This turn involved the 9.54am Waterloo to Southampton Central passenger service, returning to Nine Elms on the 5.50pm goods from Bevois Valley which the engine would work as far as Basingstoke. Dr Farmer and another visitor are visible at the end window. The DNS line to Winchester Chesil and Newbury passes behind the structure. This area is now changed beyond recognition being part of Junction 10 of the M3 with the main line passing under a concrete tunnel.

I had known of Dr Farmer for many decades – strange how coincidences work; as a young boy in the City I had been friends with the son of Dr Farmer's successor as Medical Officer of Health. I had also known of his untimely demise, indeed I had obtained a few prints I was almost certain were attributable to him but attempts to locate the family had drawn a blank.

That is until April this year when friend Ian Shawyer sent me a cutting from a recent issue of the 'Hampshire Chronicle' containing a number of images attributable to Dr Farmer. The full set of 72 were also available to view on the newspaper website. An immediate email to the Editor and a note was passed on to a daughter, Di Jeans. Mrs Jeans has been extremely helpful as indeed has Mike Vokes whom Di had originally contacted to assist in identifying several of the locations.

Unfortunately what we are missing are dates; while Di, being a young girl at the time with, she admits, no interest in trains, simply recalls some of the outings but understandably no further detail. However that may be, with grateful assistance of those mentioned, we are delighted to present a selection of views from the collection.

Lord Nelson class No. 30855 *Robert Blake* on Eastleigh duty. Duty 252 involved the 1.20pm Waterloo to Bournemouth West train and seen just leaving Brockenhurst station.

Northam station with a Western Region 53xx (possibly No. 5397) northbound with a train from Southampton terminus for Newbury/Didcot. Northam Junction signal box, with the curve to Southampton Central and Bournemouth, may be seen on the left beyond the bridge.

Meon Valley interlude. Push – pull coach set 662 operating on the Meon Valley line at Droxford. Seemingly also more railway staff than passengers.

The former Butts Junction with M7 No. 30055 heading its Meon Valley line train north towards Alton. Straight ahead is the Mid Hants route to Medstead & Four Marks and eventually Alresford (Winchester) – the term 'over the Alps' easily understood by the steep climb seen ahead. To the right is the former line to Basingstoke now just a stub siding for supplies to Treloars Hospital, the B&A having closed as a through route in 1932.

A most interesting view of shunting taking place at Privett with 700 class 0-6-0 No. 30350. Although seeming to have two platforms, that on the right had been taken out of use as far back as 1921. Subsequent to this it only ever saw occasional use for shunting purposes, the facility to cross trains here also having been curtailed.

Above: Tisted for Selborne (the latter a good three miles east of the station). We are looking south towards Privett with Farringdon (and Butts Junction) behind. The route has been closed now far longer than it was open and whilst the occupation bridge and main station buildings survive, the area of the signal box and yard behind have been given over to residential development.

Right: To commemorate the closure of two Southern branch lines, the RCTS organised the 'Hampshireman' railtour on Sunday 6 February 1955. Starting from Waterloo behind H2 No. 32421 *South Foreland*, the route was south to Guildford (via Hounslow and Chertsey), where an engine change took place. We see here the special prior to departure from Waterloo at 9.45am. Tickets for the participants showed a more accurate representation of the lines to be covered as these were printed 'Hants & West Sussex Tour' although the carriage roofboards had 'RCTS The Hampshireman' shown.

First stop Guildford where Atlantic No. 32421 came off to be replaced by E5X Nos. 32570 and 32576. Seemingly there has been a 'hurry-up' whistle as the group are heading in the same direction back to the train.

The tour continued south a short distance, taking the left fork at Peasmarsh Junction to reach Horsham. It was then south again to Hardham Junction and right on to the line to Midhurst and eventually Petersfield where the train is seen here having had another engine change. Now it was the turn of the final pairing, T9s Nos. 30301 and 30732, to take the train south to Havant, Fareham, up the Meon Valley line and eventually back to Waterloo.

Perhaps the best known of all the photo stops for the train was this one at West Meon and where water was also taken. The participants making history as being on what would be the very last train ever to traverse the full length of the MV line. We see the special train here from the road bridge that dissected the platforms, most previously published views having been taken from the embankment opposite or the platform.

A most interesting view and one that raises several questions, all unfortunately unanswered. The location is Winchester Chesil, part of the Southern Region since the regional boundary changes of 1950. The single coach train is the solitary and much modified former LSWR Directors' saloon of 1885, used in its later years as an Inspection and driver training (route familiarisation) vehicle. The working is a mystery, driver familiarity over the DNS route for Eastleigh men perhaps, except that this was usually undertaken by travelling with a crew working an actual service. The seeming lack of individuals in the saloon also tends to discount this theory. In addition the takeover was in 1950 and the BR Standard class locos were only sent to Eastleigh a few years after that date. Perhaps the most likely explanation is an inspection of the DNS line following the economies of 1955.

Boat Train at Winchester. A King Arthur class 4–6–0, believed to be No. 30789 *Sir Guy,* northbound at Winchester City with a Holland America boat train from Southampton Eastern Docks to London Waterloo. The service is passing Standard Class 4 No.76027 which has been side-tracked into the up sidings, but will shortly form the 8.57am service from Winchester to Reading.

A further boat train heading north at Winchester. This time it is thought to be No. 30855 *Robert Blake* in charge of the 'Cunarder'. This would also have been the first of one or two boat trains carrying passengers from either of the Cunard liners *Queen Mary or Queen Elizabeth* from Southampton Docks to London Waterloo station. The formation consists firstly of two baggage vans, then a number of Pullman coaches for the use of the First class passengers. B4 Class 0 – 4 – 0T No. 30083 is seen to the right on shunting duties in the goods yard.

Lord Nelson No.30851 *Sir Francis Drake* passing the old Winchester City signal box with a southbound inter–regional service, probably from the North East Region, to Bournemouth West. The engine will likely have taken over the train at Oxford.

No. 35017 *Belgian Marine* paused at Winchester City with a down working. The photograph is from the useful vantage point of Upper High Street bridge looking north. So much has changed in the ensuing years – other than the train as well. Note the signal posts appear freshly painted whilst the connection to the goods yard at this end of the station is still in place although perhaps seeing little use. The hip-roofed structure on the down side cutting was the water tank for the station water columns.

Family portrait in front of No. 35015 *Rotterdam Lloyd* at Bournemouth West.

No. 76027 just south of Eastleigh with a Bournemouth line stopping service. The mount to the right of the track prevents a view of the sheds which are immediately behind. The line on the extreme left leads from the former Stoneham sidings.

Viewed from what was then platforms 1 and 2 at Eastleigh, No. 34109 *Sir Trafford Leigh- Mallory* will shortly set off toward Chandlers Ford, Romsey and Salisbury.

Eastleigh based Class 700 No. 30306 in a siding at Winchester City awaiting departure to Alton on the 8.33am Eastleigh to Alton local freight service. The area of the sidings has been taken over for car parking for almost the past 40 years.

Family group at Farringdon (Meon Valley); after the line had been truncated as a through route.

The Dyke Branch and the Drewry and Sentinel Railcars

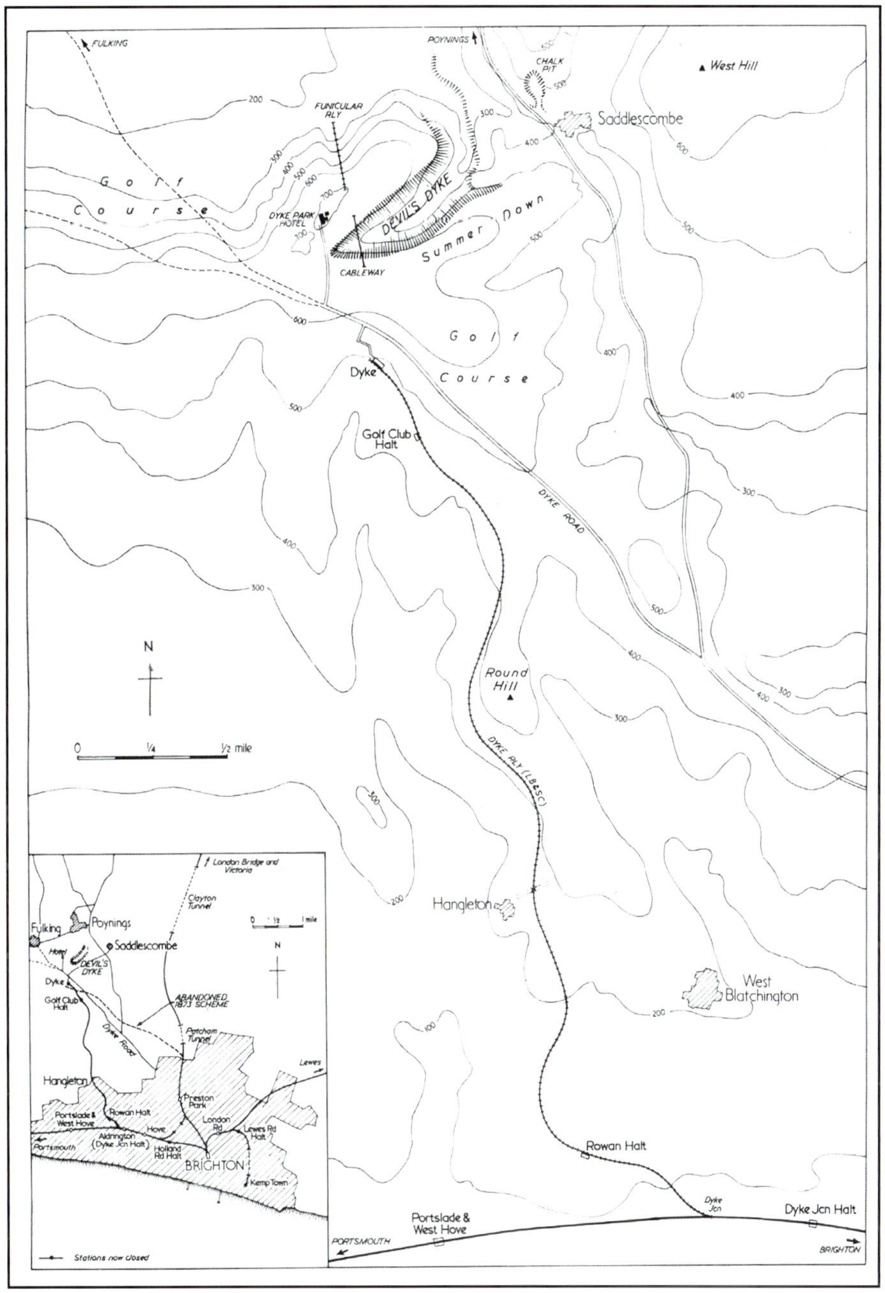

Route of the line, the line contours indicating the severity of the climb.

As enthusiasts, it is very likely certain lines or indeed subjects will hold a particular fascination in the mind. One of these, which I will admit I never knew, and indeed I doubt there are many around now who will recall its operational life, was that to the Dyke, high on the hills just to the west of Brighton.

As with almost every railway in the land, its history has been recorded previously, in the opinion of the present writer most effectively by Paul Clark in his 69 page A5 paperback ''The Railways of Devil's Dyke' published by the long defunct Turntable Publications of Sheffield in 1976.

For those without access to this recommended but now hard to find work, a brief precis of the history of the railway may be appropriate.

The name 'Dyke' is in reality a foreshortening of the full location 'Devil's Dyke', folklore having it that the Devil had been present attempting to create a cleft in the hillside to allow in the sea and so flood the villages and churches beyond the hill. He was thwarted in his task by Saint Cuthman of Steyning and also an old woman, whom Cuthman had instructed to light a taper giving the impression of impeding dawn; at which point the fiend fled although leaving a deep gouge in the hillside running due south as evidence of his attempt. (It was later recounted that in the course of construction the navvies had unearthed the skeleton of a woman considered by some to have been the individual who had worked with Saint Cuthman to defeat the Devil.)

With leisure pursuits becoming ever more important from the early 19th century onwards, the Dyke became a popular destination, its height, 712 feet, affording views south to the Isle of Wight and in the opposite direction and with the aid of a telescope it was said as far afield as Nettlebed in Oxfordshire, a distance by road of just under 86 miles but naturally a little less 'as the crow flies'.

Refreshment for visitors near the summit was first provided at an inn, according to Clark, "...in the shape of a wooden hut which had once stood on wheels near the top of Ship Street in Brighton". Later in 1831 a small inn was built on the site which would subsequently expand to become a hotel. The location attracted such notaries as royalty in the shape of William IV, plus Queen Victoria and Prince Albert, Gilbert White and Rudyard Kipling. Not surprisingly such patronage encouraged the masses although at the time the only method of vehicular transport available was a horse drawn charabanc.

A railway appears to have first been considered in the second half of the 19th century and whilst formal plans are listed as having been deposited in 1872, there would inevitably have been much discussion, possibly involving proposals that were later aborted, prior to this. It is also almost certain this 1872 proposal was at the whim of non-railway thinking people (Clark does not provide us with details of the promotors nor the estimated capital); as whilst starting on the north side of Shoreham Old Road (sic) and terminating at the Dyke, no connection is shown with the established LBSCR route at Shoreham and which immediately begs the question how might the line have been worked: locomotives, etc? Not surprisingly it did not do well in Parliament and the Bill was withdrawn through lack of support.

A second scheme was proposed in November 1873 which was in effect two railways, both reaching the Dyke but from opposing directions. One would have taken a course, with a connection into the LBSCR this time, slightly less than two miles east of Brighton station and terminated south- west of the exiting Dyke hotel. The second, again with a connection

No not taken with a drone, but instead from the top of the down home signal, a typical Edward Wallis vantage point. This is looking north into the terminus, 10 August 1924. *Edward Wallis*

On the same day we have the view of the site looking south with a train arrived but with the engine still to run round. The balloon coach at the end lives up to its name. In the first years of the branch a retired and clearly enterprising former guard set up a refreshment room on the station. *Edward Wallis*

into the LSBSCR, was from south of Patcham Tunnel facing Brighton (on the London-Brighton main line) and taking a basically westerly course to reach a similar terminus. Again we have no details of the promotors but it was clearly another independent proposition, as Clark mentions 'operating powers' over the LBSCR to Brighton. As a formal Bill it was only the first proposal, that involving a connection into the 'coastway' route that was committed to Parliament, but it too collapsed due to failed negotiations between the promoters and the two principal land-owners in the area, Lord Leconfield and the Earl of Abergavenny. As an aside both titled gentlemen were called to give evidence against the railway in Select Committee stage. This they did and promptly attempted to claim expenses for so doing – their request was declined.

It was to be a case of third time lucky, for in 1877 three individuals, William Hall of Lancing, William Hudson, a contractor from Brighton, and William Smith, a Brighton wine merchant, proposed a new Act for the Brighton and Dyke Railway which did succeed and was eventually dated 2 August 1877 although only after much 'coaxing' through Parliament. Commencing 1m 69ch west of Brighton, the new line was to be 3m 16ch long although as built it eventually extended to 3m 45ch. Capital was £72,000. To placate Lord Leconfield the little company had to agree to construct up to three bridges and a 60yd siding if required, these to be where the new line would pass through the latter's estate. Compulsory purchase powers were valid for three years with the whole undertaking to be completed in five years.

Progress however was slow, William Hudson having also departed so it was not surprising that in 1881 a set of new promotors found it necessary to secure a second Act allowing for an extension of time for completion, to 1885. The latter was not in any way unusual, numerous small schemes country-wide sometimes finding it necessary to seek an extension and for a variety of reasons. The new contractor was Henry Jackson with A. L. Nimmo as Engineer (later replaced by Charles Blabber) whilst the Hon. Ashley Ponsonby was Chairman.

Optimism now came to the fore, with estimates of passenger and goods traffic operation somewhat over-estimated. At that time, the 1880s, the population of Brighton, Hove and Preston as a whole was just 130,000 although swelled by an additional 40,000-50,000 during the summer season. (The residential population has trebled in modern times.) Figures do not appear to be given for the actual number of passengers travelling to the Dyke by road by what was then the 'large wagonettes' but we are informed the round trip occupied three hours, only one hour of this being the time spent at the actual destination. Opportunism by the operators of these vehicles was clearly also to the fore well over a century ago, as the usual fare was 1/6d although this increased by 25% to 2/d on 'special days' – the latter not defined but perhaps meaning a bank holiday or Summer weekend. By comparison, the return fare by the new railway was proposed as 2/6d, 1/8d or 1/3d according to first, second, or third class. The Brighton and Dyke railway (BDR) engineer confidently predicted 10,000 passengers would travel on a bank holiday.

Dyke station signal box, which contained a frame of 15 levers, again recorded on 10 August 1924. Originally staff and ticket had been used for working trains on the single line, but this was replaced by the Electric Train Staff from 6 October 1920. There was a local telephone circuit between the Hove station master's office, Dyke Junction and the signal box and booking office at Dyke. No intermediate sidings or passing loop was provided between the junction and the terminus. The white paint on the lower windows of the signal box was probably an attempt to reduce glare – and in summer heat – from the afternoon sun as the structure faced due west. *Edward Wallis*

Signalling diagram, undated, but fairly early as the down distant signal is still shown as a worked signal. The practice of having a working distant signal on the approach to a terminal station had been frowned upon by the Board of Trade for some time (no doubt in consequence of an incident although we do not know where). Whether the signal here was ever 'fixed' is not certain. It will be noted there are also independent rather than point discs provided. Note too the 'bay' platform is not equipped for passenger trains having no FPL on points 5.

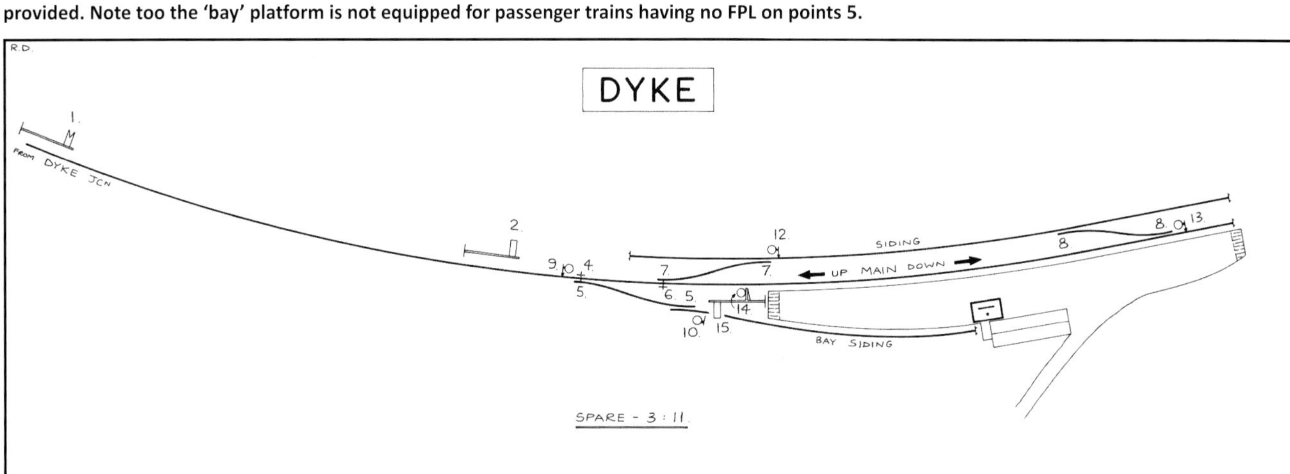

'E' class 0-6-0 No. 159, the former *Edenbridge*, on a solitary coach at the terminus. We may take this to be LBSCR days owing to the letters on the tank side. Note also the headlamps on the top of the side tank. Probable mid-week or autumn/ winter working; single coach and seemingly inclement weather. Whereas the Dyke branch lasted until the end of 1938 not so the engine which was withdrawn in January 1930.

Two points on the previous; firstly it was surely slightly unusual for an engineer to be making quotes on traffic volume, whilst in addition presumably the fares quoted related just to travel over the BDR portion of line, an additional fee payable from Brighton station (or elsewhere) as far as the junction of the line with the LBSCR.

The enthusiasm of the promoters was also such that they suggested an intermediate station be provided part way along the branch to serve Saddlescombe, Poynings, and Edburton. Possibly though such enthusiasm was not reciprocated as eventually what materialised was Golf Course Halt and even then only in 1901, some years later after the line had been in operation.

In 1882 agreement was reached between the Dyke company and the LBSCR for the latter to work the railway with receipts split 45%-55% in favour of the LBSCR. For their part of the agreement this also involved the LBSCR providing staff and for 'maintaining the stations' although it is not stated if this also included the permanent way. Interestingly the prospectus for the branch included the following, "...probably no Town in England is extending as rapidly as Brighton, such extension developing most rapidly to the north and west. The Railway will open up a district of great salubrity and beauty, and it is fair to assume that a large residential traffic will arise on a line opening up to many new and eligible sites for building." Time however would prove that this was no 'Metroland'.

At this point we will move away from the politics to more practical matters and report that the first sod was cut by Mrs Davey, in her capacity of Deputy Mayoress (sic), followed by the usual festivities and celebrations appropriate to the occasion. (Clark reports the actual sod-cutting event was repeated several times on the day in order to allow others to also participate.) At this time it was hoped the line would be completed by October 1884.

Financial difficulties would follow, investors seemingly not convinced that here was a worthwhile investment. A new Board of Directors soon followed. Recall too completion had been set in statute to be no later than 2 August 1885, a date which again proved impossible resulting in a further Act extending this to 1 June 1887 and later similar to 1 September 1887 destined to also be the date the line was at last formally opened to traffic.

Three days before this on 29 August 1887, Major General Hutchinson from the Board of Trade had inspected the works and declared the line safe to open to traffic. The first train conveying something like 30 passengers, including the contractor Henry Jackson, ran at 8.00am from Brighton on 1 September. Details of this working have survived viz; *Piccadilly,* an 0-6-0 'Terrier' tank, hauling a saloon, one first class, four third class carriages and a guard's van. The train also carried items necessary at the terminus including a clock, bell, seats and tables. (Clocks were mandatory on station platforms; if one was being carried on this inaugural working perhaps it was other than the platform clock as otherwise the Major General would surely have made comment.)

Double headed service at Dyke waiting to set off on the return to Brighton. Locomotives always faced uphill to maximise the flow of water backwards over the firebox crown. Presumably also the two engines ran round the service whilst remaining coupled. No date, but on the right hand side the bay platform appears almost derelict.

Gaiety continued with the mid-day train from Brighton on which were the VIPs, which apart from the local dignitaries included Mr William Stroudley and Mr John Saxby. Perhaps Satan did not look kindly upon the proceedings as the day was beset by rain.

A total of eight trains ran each way at first, the journey taking 20 minutes in each direction between Brighton and the Dyke inclusive of one stop at West Brighton. Trains from Brighton to the Dyke were designated as down workings, with up services running from the Dyke to Brighton. All rather confusing when it was considered down trains would be climbing up hill! The final down service was at 5.40pm.

On Sundays there were just five services in each direction, not surprisingly the first service starting later in the morning but with the final return from the Dyke as early as 6.20pm. It might have been thought that at a weekend a later service would have been provided. Fares were 1/-, 9d, and 5d single (respectively for 1st, 2nd, and 3rd class) with the corresponding returns at 1/6d, 1/2d, and 10d, all somewhat less than the comparative large wagonette service described earlier. Whether the latter continued in operation once the railway had opened is not known.

To an outsider marvelling at what would turn out to be regular crowds of trippers using the new railway the venture must have appeared an unqualified success. Indeed on the first Sunday of operation, 4 September 1887, the sale of tickets had to be temporarily suspended such was the demand. The earlier comment about the restricted Sunday service was also borne out as several additional special workings were run, this notwithstanding reports of poor weather. At this stage too the LBSCR called upon the little company to enlarge the facilities at the terminus in order to accommodate 40,000 passengers per week. Perhaps surprisingly and despite the success, the Dyke company were still inviting applications for £10,000 worth of Deferred Shares, the monies from which would have been used to provide more substantial station master's accommodation, a refreshment room, and an increase in siding space at the terminus.

Unfortunately it seems that by some the branch line was simply considered a novelty, 'travel once' perhaps rather than on a regular basis. This is based on figures for passengers carried in the first 12 months; 159,500, some way short of 273,000 which was the estimated annual total given around the same time as the 10,000 per bank holiday figure mentioned in 1882. (Whether the two estimates 10,000 and 273,000 came from the same source in 1882 is not clear.)

Any euphoria over even 159,500 would quickly turn to despair in the following years for despite passenger numbers increasing the numbers were still insufficient to cover all demands on finances and on 18 November 1895, just ten years after the tumultuous even if rather damp opening, a receiver was appointed for the BDR. Even so it would continue to 'trade' in this form until absorbed by the Southern Railway from 22 July 1924.

From 1905 pull-push trains were introduced comprising 'Balloon' vehicles although supplemented by ordinary stock according to demand. This type of operation ceased sometime after 1920 – possibly commensurate with the reopening (see below) after which the working instructions required locomotives always to run on the line with the chimney facing towards the Dyke terminus. This would also ensure the water in the boiler would cover the firebox crown on the uphill stretches – of which there were many – of the branch. No watering facilities for engines were provided at the Dyke terminus.

There was a temporary closure of the line from 1 January 1917 until 26 July 1920 for basic economy reasons during what were difficult times, but unlike some other lines which suffered a similar fate, for the Dyke branch, the track remained *in situ*. From July 1924 until final closure on 31 December 1938 the Southern Railway was in charge. Under their watch a second stopping place was provided from 12 January 1934. This was Rowan Halt, intended to serve nearby housing developments

Believed to be E4 No. 2505 having arrived and before running round. From the shadows, an early afternoon working. After running round there was a standing instruction to test the brake before commencing any journey from Brighton or indeed Dyke – but surely that was a normal requirement anyway?

but also destined to be the termination point for around half the branch trains in the last winters of operation.

As might be expected, traffic on the branch was primarily passenger, less so of course in winter, although the first train to the terminus in the morning operated as a mixed service, the last vehicle being a goods brake van under the control of a goods guard. On this train the traffic might well be coal, coke and cattle food plus various small consignments. In addition parcels were handled at the terminus, the latter delivered by the local coal merchant who was paid 1d per delivery. Outward goods traffic was mainly baled straw and hay. Goods traffic however ceased from 2 January 1933 when the siding at the terminus was taken out of use.

The final timetable, covering the period Winter 1934, showed eight trains on weekdays running through to (and returning from) the Dyke, whilst a further nine operated only as far as Rowan Halt. Eight services operated on Sundays, all covering the whole line. All of these were also now one-class only.

The demise of the branch was in effect a combination of circumstances affecting not just the Dyke branch but other Southern lines and indeed certain lines from other companies as well. Competition allied to the flexibility of road travel meant it was just as easy, if not easier, to reach the Dyke by road. Traffic during summer may well have been attractive but the winter months invariably meant operating expenses far exceeded revenue. It was the reverse situation of Dr Beeching a quarter of a century later, peaks and troughs of line usage rather than stock usage, even so the result was the same. Closure took effect from 31 December 1938.

The line described

From Dyke Junction, the branch climbed continuously, starting at a leisurely 1 in 281 and 1 in 316 before quickly steepening with a short section of 1 in 81 and then climbing at 1 in 40/ 1 in 41 for almost the rest of the journey. Indeed, even the intermediate halts and the terminus were on a gradient, the latter on 1 in 391. Neither was this a steady climb as there were numerous sharp curves, the tightest at just 13 chains close to the main line junction and the least of 30 chain radius.

Under such circumstances it is perhaps not unusual to relate, although perhaps hard to understand perhaps a century or more ago, that folklore dictates some trains travelled so slowly on the ascent that passengers would alight and walk alongside picking fruit from the hedgerows. The crews would also return gingerly, the train stopping to put out fires caused by sparks from the engine on the way up to the terminus. There are also stories of the train having to stop to clear snow from the line during winter.

Near the Dyke terminus was the hotel previously mentioned; it was destroyed by fire some years after the line closed but subsequently rebuilt. There was also an aerial cableway and funicular railway although both are outside the remit of this article.

An undated view of a chalk fall covering the head shunt at the Dyke terminus. Was this even a regular occurrence perhaps? The consequence would have been to make it difficult if not impossible to run round although from the photograph it is not possible to exactly determine how much space remained. Possible 'top and tail' working ensued for a time.

In 1891 Golf Course Halt was opened and located just 62 chains from the terminus, serving the Brighton and Hove golf course, one of three clubs to have links nearby. Facilities (at the halt not the course!) were a single brick platform of 'substantial length' plus a nameboard. Interestingly no illumination was provided. Perhaps the railway considered trains would only ever be required to call during daylight hours but then they had forgotten to consider the 'nineteenth' hole. The stopping place was in effect a private station as the name never appeared in the public timetable. Consequently, golfers had to book a ticket to and from Dyke station. A slightly strange instruction from the LBSCR Appendix to the Working Instructions appears in 1917, "A platform at the Golf Club House is in use for passengers to join or leave trains, but the Station masters, at Brighton, Hove and the Dyke, as well as the guards, must take care that no train, *unless it is carrying the train staff*, is stopped at this platform to take up or set down passengers" – the emphasis in italics is that of the present writer as surely every train on what was a single line would have to carry the train staff anyway.

In order to advise golfers who wished to join a train travelling back towards Brighton that a service was due, an electric bell was installed in the club house which was actuated upon the Dyke starting signal being pulled to its 'off' position. The club also appeared to have carried some weight with the LBSCR as various suggestions made relative to changing the times of trains 'for the convenience of members' were in the whole acceded to. A shelter was also proposed, the railway stating this would cost £100, but it is not believed this was in fact ever built. In darkness golfers wishing to join the train might light a match to advise the driver to stop.

Dyke Junction Halt was located, as the name implies, at the junction on the main line with the branch. Here, there were up and down platforms, its opening coinciding with the opening of three other local halts (unrelated to the Dyke branch) but related to the introduction of a 'motor' service between Brighton and Worthing. Dyke Junction Halt was renamed Aldrington in June 1932 and remains open for Coastway services today.

Rowan Halt has already been mentioned and proved to be popular with workers travelling home from Brighton at lunch time although a study of the timetables would tend to indicate anyone so participating may have been entitled to slightly more than one hour's break mid-day. Paul Clark also makes mention of a fake 'Hangleton Halt' invented by a somewhat less than scrupulous estate agent in an attempt to sell houses further up the line.

Despite its definitely lowly branch line status, engines of various sizes, including tender types, were recorded on the branch. Regular performers included E4 and D1 tanks whilst even the I1X and I2 engines appeared as well as C2 and C2X classes, the latter on ballast trains.

Criticism was made at times of the lack of late evening services on the line but this is explained when the opening times of the signal boxes at Dyke Junction and Dyke for 1922 are considered.

Dyke Junction: weekdays 9.55am to 5.55pm. Sunday 9.45am to 12.50pm and 2.20pm to 5.45pm.

Dyke: weekdays 10.26am to 5.30pm. Sunday 10.16am to 5.30pm.

Both boxes were shown as closed during the winter.

The point here being that even with a split shift at the junction box in winter, the working would involve just one man without the need for overtime or a relief. Slightly strange, though, that mention is made of both boxes being closed in winter which implies there were no Sunday trains in the Winter period.

Bleak day, bleak location, the station building reminiscent even of contemporary Colonel Stephens station structures. Again the disparity in vehicle heights will be noted. As an independent company full of hope there were provisional expansion plans from the Dyke to reach Henfield (6 miles) on the Steyning line, or the shorter distance to Fulking plus the provision of a station at Hangleton. Whether these were formal representations or merely expansive dreams is not certain as none came to fruition.

Paul Clark was fortunate in his book to be able to reproduce the results of interviews carried out with staff who had been involved with the railway. At the time of publication of his book, 1976, it was slightly less than 40 years since the last trains had run, today obtaining such recollections would be impossible. Mr L. Budd for example was, in 1929/30, occupying the role of signalman, booking clerk and shunter at the Dyke working from 9.55am to 5.55pm and travelling to work on the first train. This involved leaving the staff out the previous evening for the driver to collect as he passed Dyke Junction with the first train of the morning. To achieve this meant the final departure from the Dyke in the previous evening would have been verbally instructed to pass the down starting signal at danger, the up home having been pulled off ready for the next day.

Mr Budd also recalled the time when the staff dropped off the engine on the way back to the junction. Considerable delay was incurred whilst a second staff was released by a linesman (to return the instruments to the correct phase) whilst in addition an inspector had to walk the line to physically confirm it was indeed clear of any other train. He continued that on some occasions whilst on duty at the terminus, he would only see the train crew all day, there being no passengers.

The Drewry and Sentinel railcars

Whilst some closed lines wither away, to be recalled only by a few individuals, the Dyke branch has remained a better known name, likely due to its use with the pioneering Sentinel steam railcar which operated the line between 1933 and early 1936.

Unlike the LNER, which was a prolific user of Sentinel products both as shunters and as passenger railcars, No. 6, as it was known on the Southern, was destined to be a 'one-off'. The GWR had also used a Sentinel 0-4-0 locomotive briefly for trials hauling the passenger services on the Malmesbury branch but this was not pursued.

The railcar story on the Southern really commences in 1927 when a Drewry railcar was ordered with the intention of securing economy in branch line operation over lines where in future electrification might not be viable. Delivered around March 1928 the vehicle was powered by a 50hp petrol engine and could accommodate 26 passengers. Initially gearbox issues plagued the design but once these were resolved, the vehicle operated a regular service between Andover and Romsey; that is, until its success in generating extra traffic overwhelmed its carrying capacity. It subsequently worked between Reading

Left: **From the 'Southern Railway Magazine' of 1933, the Drewry petrol car is seen entering Ashford whilst on trial between Ashford, Appledore and New Romney.**

Below: **In its later, and final life, the same vehicle on the WC&P, this time with trailer attached.** *Mike King*

and Blackwater and on Appledore-New Romney-Dungeness services. Following a breakdown in February 1930 the vehicle entered Ashford Works where the engine was uprated to 64hp but it was also noted the seating capacity had been reduced to 22. Whether the engine change had contributed towards the reduced capacity or the change was perhaps to allow more luggage/ parcels to be carried is not stated. Its subsequent life on the Southern is not reported but it was noted at Bristol in July 1934 en route to the Weston, Clevedon & Portishead railway. Whether the vehicle might have been considered a sound investment for the Southern is perhaps debatable, especially as the reported purchase price in 1927/8 was said to have been £1,810 whilst when it was sold to the WC&P this was for just £272. (In its new home the vehicle remained at work until WW2. It was subsequently scrapped three months after the GWR purchased the WC&P line in June 1940.)

Whilst we may state categorically that No. 5 did not work on the Dyke branch, Railcar No. 6 most certainly did. No. 6 was a Sentinel steam railcar. Bradley refers to it as being of Sentinel-Cammell type completed in March 1933, specifically it appears for use on the Dyke branch. Clearly the advantages of the railcar design still appealed to the SR; a solitary driver was possible with the Sentinel design even though it was steam-powered and coal-fired. Unfortunately it appears the principal lesson learnt from the Drewry experience was either ignored or simply forgotten and which was that this type of vehicle would likely generate additional traffic and yet the Sentinel design was incapable of satisfying any additional demand as it was not designed and indeed not capable of taking a trailing load. (The GWR learnt the same, their first 'streamlined' diesel cars having to be replaced by locomotive hauled trains commensurate with demand. Later GWR single cars were designed so that they might take a limited trailing load as traffic required.)

Returning to the Southern, it was reported in Bradley that No. 6 left Birmingham (the Sentinel works were in Shrewsbury, whereas what was later Metropolitan-Cammell was in Birmingham) on 19 June to travel under its own power to Brighton via Northampton and Willesden Junction. Dependent upon the source quoted, Clark, Bradley, or Holcroft, a speed of 60mph was obtained at mile post 74 just south of Long Buckby between Kilsby and Northampton. Even at speed coal and water consumption were reasonable, just 4¾cwt of coal used on the 109 mile run to Willesden the equivalent of 4.88lbs per mile (the hopper type coal bunker held 5cwt). Water usage was equally frugal at 318 gallons equivalent to 2.92 gallons per mile. Holcroft adds to the detail and from this source we are told that three water stops were made,

Official view of Sentinel Car No. 6. The vehicle was destined to remain a prototype, the result of a combined effort by Sentinel, the Doble steam car company of California, and Metropolitan Cammell. It is possible the external design of the body owed more to Doble than MC, its appearance being markedly similar to contemporary American streamline railway design. No doubt originally intended as a demonstrator, in the event the vehicle was purchased outright by the Southern Railway for £2,680 perhaps implying that the Sentinel company had been unable to persuade other railway companies to consider the vehicle. *Mike King*

at Rugby No. 5 (signal box), Bletchley and Willesden. A stop was also made at Tring to fill the lubricator. Water capacity was 240 gallons, contained in a well tank. Provision was made for the tank capacity to be increased by a further 50% to 360 gallons although we are not told if this was in fact even undertaken. Certainly as a branch type vehicle a run in excess of 100 miles would not be what the vehicle had been intended for.

Holcroft was on board for the delivery run, the vehicle driven by Abner Doble whose steam engine design was being used in the railcar. Somewhat unusual too that the American was permitted to drive the machine on a British railway albeit with a pilotman from the LMS, who boarded after the car left Metro-Cammell at Washwood Heath. The trip south started at 7.43am, Doble continued driving to Willesden and indeed on to Brighton later. For the second half of the run an SR pilotman was provided. The whole delivery episode seems to have been almost a jolly affair as after arrival at Willesden at 11.10am there was an "...interval for lunch..." with departure for the Southern made at 12.16pm.

The journey on to Brighton had been booked to take 2hrs 53 minutes and was completed in one minute less despite a succession of signal checks between Wandsworth Common and Selhurst and a further water stop at Haywards Heath. We are not told where the water filler was located on the vehicle but with the railcar equipped with a well tank it tends to imply this would have been low down – interesting then that the hose from a standard water column could thus be used?

From a technical perspective the vehicle was 48ft 8ins in length, 8 feet in width and 11 feet high. The body was carried on two lightweight bolster bogies. The engine part of the vehicle was a 97hp compound steam engine, the high pressure cylinder being 4½ inch diameter and the low pressure cylinder 7½ diameter, both cylinders shared a common 6 inch stroke. Stephenson Link motion was fitted operating piston valves, all the working parts being enclosed in what Paul Clark refers to as an 'oil chamber'; Mr Bulleid would probably have said an 'oil bath'. The whole was of diminutive size and small enough to be arranged horizontally and also nose-suspended between the bogie wheels. Drive was to a single axle by a series of gears. Also beneath the floor was a battery for electric lighting charged, it is believed, by a generator when the vehicle was in motion. Despite just a single axle being driven there are no reports of issues with wheel slip.

Again from the 'SR Magazine' we see the vehicle brand new inside Brighton Works and what is probably a trial trip at Dyke. Unlike its steam engine counterparts the accompanying images show that the car ran with both the chimney facing and chimney trailing on the branch.

Running on the electrified coast line at Aldrington Halt, 11 August 1933. According to 'SR Magazine' the seats are 'decidedly comfortable' – but then they were probably duty bound to say that. It was to keep out of the way of the electric services on this section that Maunsell choose what, in the opinion of others, was the wrong gear ratio for the vehicle. True it could certainly run at speed but its ability to climb the steeply graded Dyke branch was therefore compromised. *H. C. Casserley/Mike King*

One unusual aspect was the design of the wheels and brakes. The wheels were made with wooden centres, akin to the Maunsell type (note: no connection here with the SR CME Maunsell). This was intended to provide for quieter running. Electrical conductivity to ensure the vehicle could activate track circuits was provided by introducing a strip of copper from the tyres to the hubs – the latter attached to the axles and with roller bearings on the axles. Braking was by drums attached to the outside of the wheels. Drum brakes were then and indeed continued to be the standard form of braking on road vehicles for many years and in this way the connection with both the Sentinel and Doble companies with their respective steam road vehicles comes to the fore. By placing the drums 'outboard' there was also excellent cooling available and the chances of fade – where the drum expands away from the brake shoes due to heat generated through friction – was reduced. The actual brakes were operated by a steam cylinder and rodding.

Above the floor was a standard Sentinel design road wagon vehicle boiler pressed to 325lbs psi. An automatic feed-water regulator maintained a constant water level whilst the automatic stoker was controlled by the same pump through a ratchet mechanism and a screw. The coal bunker was physically located above the level of the boiler which was filled through an upper door. Coal and water were linked in a fixed ratio and it was this automation that allowed the car to be driven with confidence by one man from either end. Even so there remain questions of detail, how was coal taken on board, and presumably the coal used had to be limited to a certain size to prevent blockages. No mention has been found of an oil-firing alternative.

The body could accommodate 44 passengers in two separate saloons, one of 24, the other of 20. Each was accessed via a centre door on either side of the car although doors at either end were also provided for driver and guard. Seating was in bucket type seats, cushions filled with Dunlop latex and upholstered in moquette, all turned to face towards the centre passage/doors. No couplings or buffers were provided but there were 'bumper bars' at each end. The interior was steam-heated.

Total weight was just under 17 tons, with a slight disparity to the right-hand side of 12cwt due to the positioning of the water tank and battery box.

After arrival at Brighton on 19 March 1933 and inspection, some trial trips were made between Brighton and Steyning for the benefit of drivers who would later be in charge. In addition, two trial runs were made on the Dyke branch starting and terminating at Brighton. It is not known how many were involved for the first run on the branch but 20 were taken on the second trip. The runs were arranged to replicate a normal service. In both cases the net time was less than the normal steam service. The vehicle consumed 40 gallons of water on each of the down (uphill) trips and respectively 15 and 23 gallons on the return runs. Although satisfactory, some difficulty was experienced with the coal used due to the sticky nature of what was a mix of Chislet and hard supplies. On such a steeply graded line the brakes were of paramount importance but these were perfectly satisfactory even when the vehicle was overloaded with standing passengers. In view of the comment about the coal used it may well have been that specific types of coal were used later.

The following day, 24 March, a trial was made from Brighton as far as Southwater, back to Steyning, return to Southwater and finally back to Brighton. On one of these a maximum speed of 66mph was obtained, possibly the fastest the car ever travelled. This was despite there being a 45mph speed restriction in force owing to the state of the p/way between Shoreham Junction and Itchingfield Junction; the vehicle's light weight and lack of hammer blow meaning the Divisional Engineer was content to waive the normal restriction.

At the terminus on 10 October 1933 with the compartment opposite the boiler end clearly showing the word 'Luggage' written on the door. Not mentioned in any of the official reports but it appears it may have had electric lights fitted. The purpose of what appears to be the pipe hanging down ahead of the left hand front wheel is not reported. *Mike King*

Further trials were made on 28 March when the 3½ miles of the actual branch were climbed in 8-8½ minutes. As a result of the tests some minor alterations were found desirable; a screen to protect the driver from heat from the boiler, speedometers, bell communication between driver and guard, and sand pipe guards to prevent sand being blown away from the rails by crosswinds. The volume of the horn (the word is specifically used rather than the term 'whistle') was adjusted and the passenger seats raised. A further proposal for a sliding panel in the roof to assist ventilation above the boiler was deferred and, it is believed, never carried out. Initial concern over efficiency of the brakes was also discounted although larger diameter drums were later fitted by the manufacturer. Further trials followed from 11 April. Holcroft speaks of five runs but we cannot be certain if these were in fact all on the same day.

In similar vein, A. G. Perryman, in his biography 'Life at Brighton Works' (Oakwood Press 1972), gives us his opinion and experiences of the vehicle. ". . . the authorities decided to acquire a 'Sentinel' Railcar for operating the branch which ran up to the Devils Dyke. Upon delivery, this car had to do a certain mileage before it could be handed over to public service, and quite a few troubles befell it, and it made many visits to the works for sundry adjustments. After one such visit, Henry had inquired of the driver if it were possible to have a ride on it to the Dyke and back. He was told that if he liked to get over to the shed one day just before it left, and get aboard without being seen, he, the driver, would have no objection.

Unusual angle alongside the terminus station, 11 October 1933. Notice the cover available atop the chimney. *H. C. Casserley/Mike King*

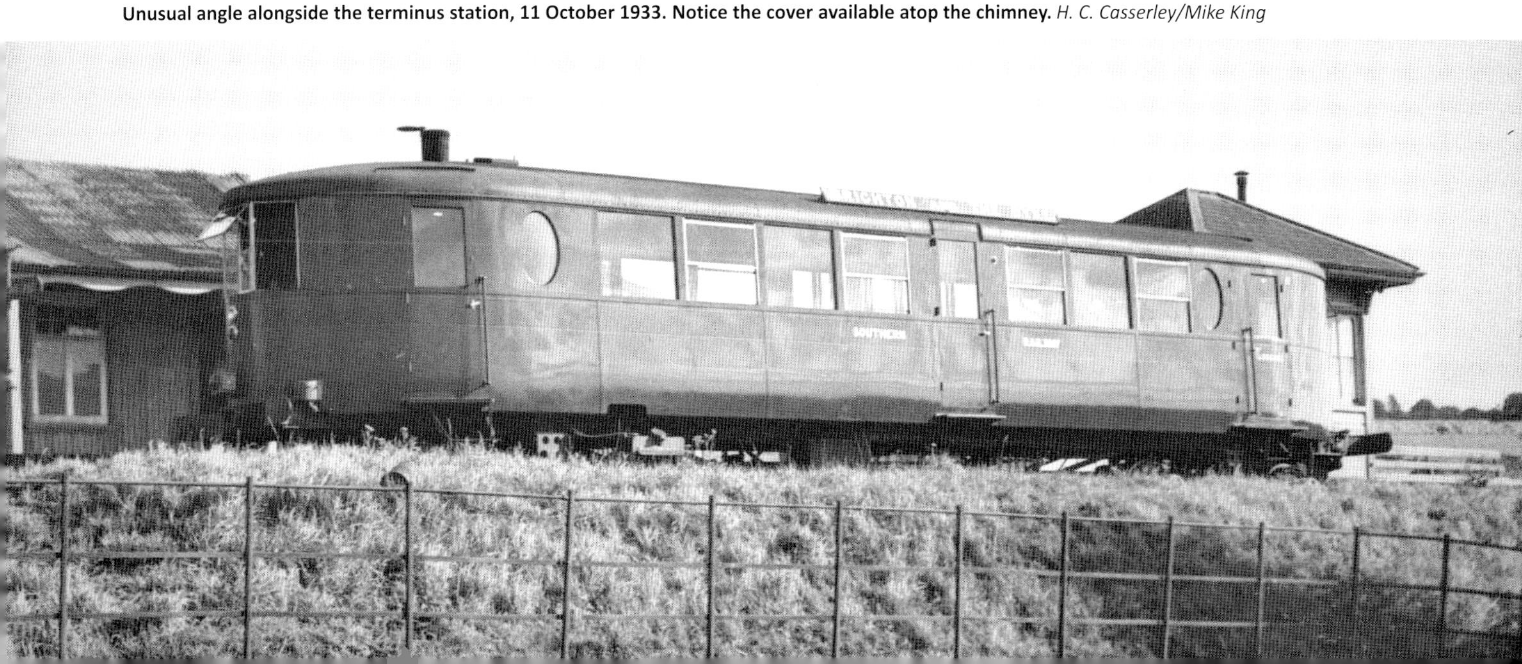

New(ish) condition by the water softener at Brighton. Whatever advantage the car may have had was also negated by the need for it to be serviced in a steam depot environment. Is that also a few dents on the front corner panelling...? *Mike King*

"Henry mentioned this to me and suggested that I should go along with him for moral support. It was duly agreed between us, so one fine day we both managed to slip away without being seen, and crossed the main lines to the shed. We found the railcar in the yard, and Henry had a few words with the driver, who told him the departure time. We were told to join it just as he was about to start, and keep out of sight, this we did, and off we went! This was very different to my first trial run. Here was no noise or vibration at all, just the clicking of the wheels over the rail joints, no exhaust beat to speak of, just a purr of the multi-cylinder engine. I believe it was a single acting multi, very similar to the one used on the firm's steam road lorry, and was supplied by a vertical, high pressure boiler. It made heavy going of the climb up to the Dyke, and upon arrival the driver left his cab and proceeded to the other end to the controls in a second cab at that end. Henry and I had got out on the platform for a stretch and nearly got left behind, as the driver was off again in a few moments. We should have been stranded up at that lonely outpost for heaven knows how long, as it was only making infrequent runs, at no set times. However, we did manage to get back on board and the trip back was much quicker as it was all downgrade. Upon approaching the works and yard, we were told to keep out of sight once more, and to leave it, on shed, without being seen. We thanked the driver and departed. No one ever said anything about it, so I suppose we weren't spotted.

"We arrived back in the works, having been missing for about a couple of hours, but we apparently hadn't been missed, and no one even asked where we'd been.

"There was quite a bit of trouble with the brakes on this car. It had large cast iron drums bolted on outside the wheels, with large air cooling holes in their sides. The shoes were lined with linings similar to car brakes of the period. Sentinel's men came down to modify these brakes in the works and I got talking to them. They told me that the fault was really with the Southern's operating department. The car was supplied with a choice of three gear ratios, and the request was for the highest of the three, to give a top speed of nearly 60 mph on the level, as they didn't want it to delay the newly-introduced electric service between Brighton Central and Aldrington Halt, where the Dyke branch left the main line. The makers had advised the lowest set of gears in view of the heavy climb from Aldrington to the Dyke, but the company would have the highest. Consequently the car frequently stalled on the grade and had to stand still for a 'blow up'. Worse still, on the descent, there was not so much retarding effect from the engine in the higher gear, so the brakes had to do all the work. They got very hot in the process and the car had been known to sail straight through Aldrington Halt non-stop and only succeeded in stopping at Hove with the greatest difficulty! Wider drums and brake shoes were fitted, and this did help a lot, but it was usually touch and go coming down, if there was much of a load on. The car did eventually go into service, but did not last very long. It was not designed to take a trailer at busy times, so could not satisfy the traffic demands. It was eventually transferred to the Westerham branch in Kent, and the radial 0-6-2 tanks with one or two coaches reinstated."

The vehicle entered public service on 1 May 1933 painted in Southern green with ownership lettering centrally on the side and a roofboard either side proclaiming 'Brighton and The Dyke' in gold lettering.

In service the car mostly worked with the boiler end leading on the branch. Unfortunately the lack of any brake blocks on the wheels – which in effect also scrubbed the tyres when the brakes were in use – meant the wheel tyres could become dirty and so cause a wrong-side track-circuit failure. (This is where the track-circuit does not detect the presence of a vehicle.) The problem was solved by the simple expedient of occasional pressure washing of the wheels.

Recorded at Tonbridge during the short time the vehicle worked in the area. The in board axle bearings are reminiscent of some modern day rolling stock. Likewise the brakes, although nowadays more efficient discs are used. *Mike King*

Whilst published accounts, including that of the late H. Holcroft ('Locomotive Adventure' Volume 2, Ian Allan 1965) tend to paint a relatively rosy image of the vehicle in service, the same is not reported by A. C. Perryman who was at Brighton Works at the time. Mr Perryman comments that the gear ratio was really unsuited for the branch and its gradients, yet the SR had specifically stipulated the ratios so as to allow the railcar to run at a reasonable speed and so keep clear of the electric service between Brighton and Dyke Junction. It was this unsuitable ratio that was the cause of the vehicle either stalling or being unable to make much headway on the steep gradients. In the reverse direction the brakes were called into question and when they overheated on more than one occasion the vehicle was unable to stop at the junction and continued on to Hove. In view of the early comments concerning the satisfactory nature of the brakes when the car was first delivered this is strange and the only comments we can make are perhaps the vehicle was being driven at an excess speed on the downhill or the brake shoes had become worn so there was less friction contact with the drums – unless of course this was also the reason for the increased diameter brake drums referred to earlier?

Despite such issues the vehicle was popular but suffered the same fate as other railcars in that it was incapable of hauling a trailer. As such the vehicle worked weekday trains on the branch but on Saturday afternoon and Sunday services, a two-coach steam service was substituted.

Moving away from the Dyke, in August 1933 two Sundays were spent working between Horsham and Three Bridges and another on the Westerham branch. These trials were successful as in February the following year Maunsell recommended the purchase of five additional vehicles, two to work Staines – Ascot – Camberley – Aldershot, and one each for the Horsham – Three Bridges and Westerham branch services. The fifth vehicle would be spare and also cover services on the Dyke branch as necessary. 'Traffic' also wished for an increase in passenger capacity with 65 seats and even suggested a two-car arrangement.

Harry Holcroft included this delightful view of the car climbing near to the terminus.

As a result trials were made with a Clayton car seating 64, and a Sentinel twin with 54 seats but neither were considered suitable. An alternative was offered by ArmstrongWhitworth in the form of a twin diesel-electric set but this disgraced itself by catching fire whilst on test. The cause of the railbus was not helped when a quote was received from Sentinel for vehicles to the specification set by Maunsell and which came in far higher than had been expected. Consequently by early 1935 and with no progress made thoughts turned away from railcars and back to conventional steam pull-push workings and electrification.

So far as No. 6 was concerned, it continued in service on the Dyke branch until 1 May 1935 when it was taken out of service owing to a fractured bogie bolster. It was repaired but never worked to the Dyke again, this was due to the Traffic Department commenting that the vehicle was unable to deal with the volume of passengers. For some months therefore, No. 6 simply stood idle.

Its history post 1936 is simply explained. Traffic considered it might well now find a use on the Westerham branch from Dunton Green and trials were initially arranged from Tonbridge as well as on the branch itself.

Whilst no comment has been found relative to the views of drivers whilst it was based at Brighton it was a different situation at Westerham. Drivers now insisted a fireman be present for the main line part of the journey to and from Dunton Green. Strange no such issues had been raised when running between Dyke Junction and Brighton. In addition its reputation that it would regularly stall on the climb soon after the Hildenborough stop did not find favour with early morning commuters who were delayed as a consequence. Soon after it became practice for the car to be piloted between Tonbridge and Dunton Green; but this immediately raises the question, how were the two coupled? Another criticism was that the vehicle itself was affected by wind, complaints allegedly received from both passengers and the driver – although in view of previous comments we may even wonder if the latter even encouraged such opinion among others. Whilst working on the Westerham branch, any defect that occurred would result in a fitter having to be sent from Tonbridge and the service suspended in the meanwhile. At night it was also stabled in the yard at Tonbridge where there was no choice but to stand it amongst the dirt and grime of the steam engines – exactly the same scenario as had beset the steam railmotors proper a generation earlier. Once more none of these issues appear to have been realised or considered a difficulty when working from Brighton.

In October 1936 the vehicle moved away and spent some days on the Hawkhurst branch and in November was used for evening trains between Tunbridge Wells and Edenbridge. Clearly also the novelty had worn off, as the days spent out of service increased although on 22 April 1937 it was rostered for a Tunbridge Wells West working. With only a limited number of passengers the journey to High Brooms was uneventful but a major failure occurred on the return whilst crossing Colebrook viaduct. Here the railcar stuck until "fitters arrived to dismantle the engine" a comment from Bradley but which may have a direct bearing on what is mentioned later. (Paul Clark refers to a 'boiler failure' having occurred and this might seem to be borne out by the comments of Mr Bulleid later, but it does not fit in with the need for 'fitters to dismantle the engine'.)

Evidently heat for the driver might well have been an issue as per the front window open. (Implying the suggested roof vent was never in fact fitted.) Holcroft also makes the valid suggestion it was a shame it could not have been repaired and modified, perhaps as an Engineer's inspection vehicle, when its revenue earning days were over.

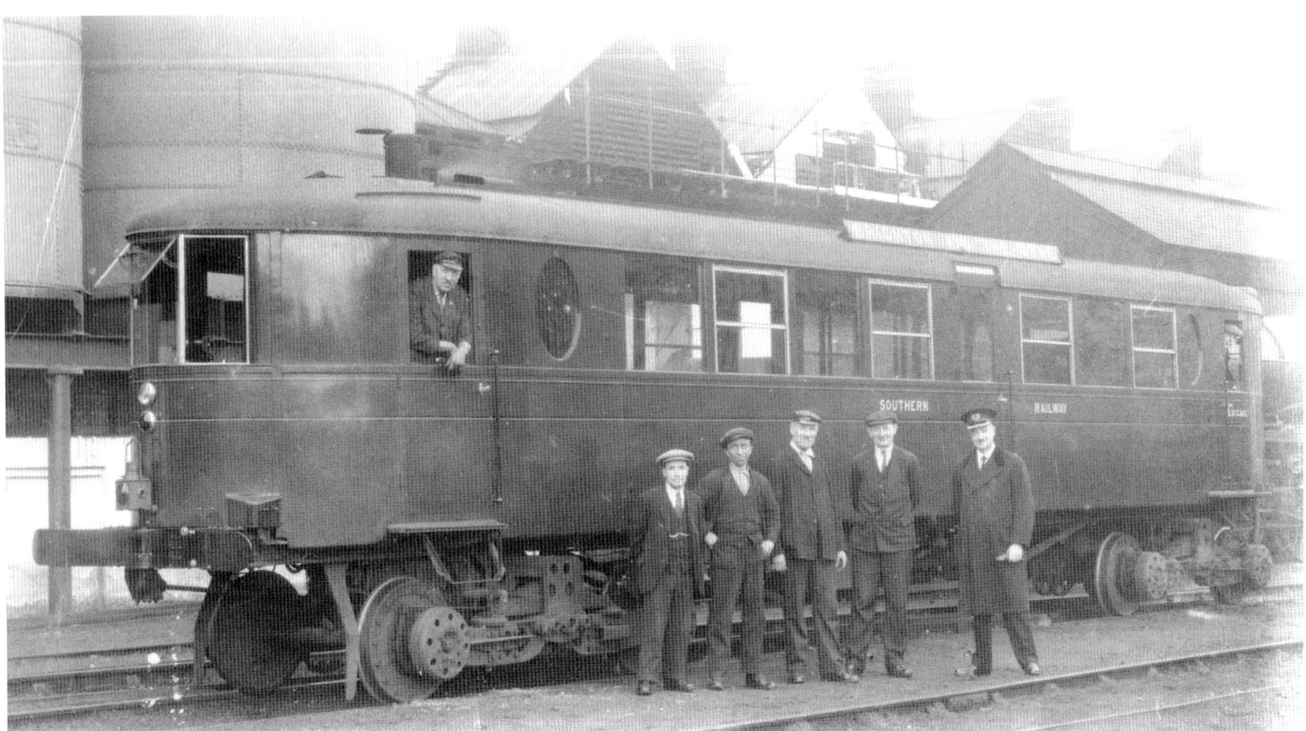

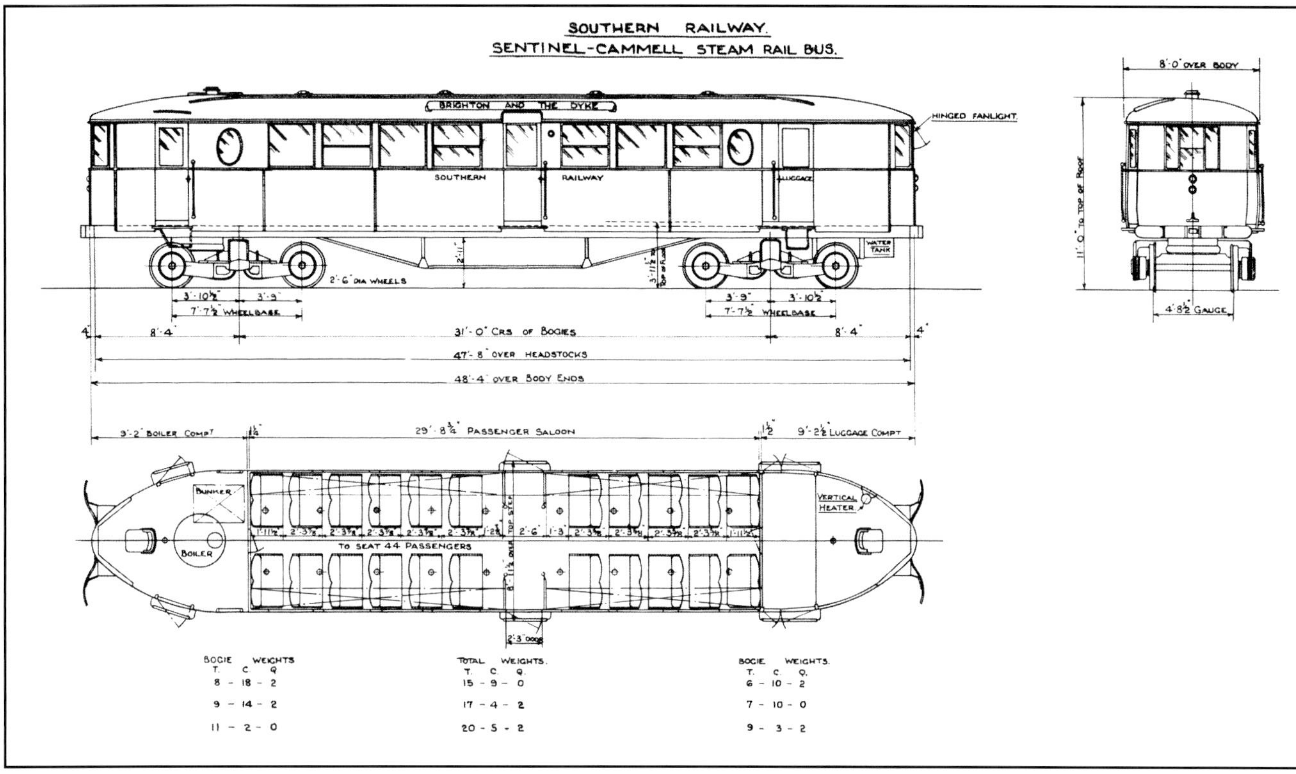

The car was subsequently towed to Ashford where it was noted in June 1938 having previously been stored at Tonbridge shed. The intention was for it to be repaired and put to use on the Gravesend West branch. Unfortunately inspection of the boiler saw this condemned with Bulleid, now in charge as CME, considering the expense of repair/replacement unjustified. It was then again stored, this time in the Ashford paint shop pending a decision.

In September 1940 the vehicle was stripped, the body painted dull grey, taken outside and used as messing facilities for the works Home Guard and Fire Watchers. Initially it was placed outside the Brass Shop but it later moved to a new position outside the Wheel Shop. It was still present in April 1946 but with hostilities at an end it was now no longer required and was slowly dismantled during the autumn of 1946. Official withdrawal had not been until January 1942.

There the story might have ended except for the actual engine unit. Around the same time C. H. Hutchinson at Brighton was one of those involved with the ongoing development of what would turn out to be the 'Leader' design. Bulleid, as we know, was toying with any number of ideas at that time, a high speed steam engine for the drive being just one of these. Hutchinson recalled the railcar and its engine and made enquiries as to whether the engine part actually still survived. It did and accordingly the engine was removed to Brighton for inspection. What happened next is not clear but it matters not, as no progression was subsequently made in this direction. Unsuitable for use in Leader no doubt – output as much as anything else – but also perhaps unsuitable to even trial as an idea for development, perhaps even due to its earlier failure on Colebrook viaduct. In his own narrative Holcroft had commented "The one item that never gave any trouble was the engine", but whether he was involved and had knowledge of the vehicle throughout its life is not totally clear.

Bibliography and Acknowledgement

'Locomotive Adventure Vol 2'. H. Holcroft Ian Allan 1965

'Locomotives of the Southern Railway Part 1'. D. L. Bradley. Published RCTS 1975

'The Railways of Devil's Dyke'. Paul Clark. Turntable Publications 1976

'The Southern Railway Magazine' 1933

The author also gratefully acknowledges the help of Mike King.

The S. C. Townroe Archive – in Colour
Part 5

For this issue's selection we have moved (temporarily) away from steam and on to the time of the big diesels on the Southern as occurred in the early 1950s.

As ever, what involvement SCT had with the type we cannot be certain although we know he did at least ride on one of the Southern variants, and probably the LMS design. There is no evidence any ever visited Eastleigh – passed through at the head of the Bournemouth Belle certainly, but otherwise fuelling was undertaken on a siding outside Waterloo whilst they were also looked after at Nine Elms and repaired as necessary at Brighton.

Unfortunately we cannot later continue the non-steam theme in the future with electric types and for the simple reason there are none, apart that is from a COR being painted in blue in the Eastleigh carriage works. Instead No. 57 will see a bit of a main line surprise: the big engines and the big scenes. What can I say other than roll on No. 57!

Above: **April 1953 and service time at Eastleigh. M7 No. 30379 is being serviced outside the front of the shed; slightly unusual location for this to be carried out and which seems to involve some tube cleaning as well. Alongside is 350hp diesel-electric No. 15230, one of a batch of 26 engines built at Ashford between 1949 and 1952. They were based on the earlier SR design but with Bulleid wheels and detail alterations copied from the LMS shunters. It might thus be said to be an early example of inter-regional co-operation. Even so servicing in the open was still far from ideal. With the end of the (steam) oil burning story in 1948/9 there was some discussion about converting the former boiler house at Eastleigh into a diesel shunter maintenance facility but this did not take place. No. 30379 had a life of 59 years being withdrawn from Three Bridges in 1963. No. 15230 was one of the final members of the class to be withdrawn in 1971 after a life of 20 years, the class by now designated BR Class 12, becoming extinct in the same year. No. 15230 was cut up at Cashmore's, Newport, the following year.**

Opposite top: **During the time the LMS twins, 10000 and 10001, were at work on the Southern Region, refuelling was undertaken by the simple expedient of gravity feed from a tank wagon strategically placed in the sidings outside Waterloo – at least compared with a steam engine it did not have to make its way to Nine Elms. Despite this advantage it appears from the look of the footplateman alongside he is perhaps none too impressed with the new traction. No definite confirmation as to which twin the engine might be but most likely 10000.**

Bottom: **Passing Woodfidley in the New Forest with what SCT refers to as the 'Sunday Belle' sometime in 1953. Twelve cars make up the tare load, perhaps 480 tons, and gross something a bit over 500 tons – a fair train for a 1,600hp engine.**

Nº2

Same location but this time we are told April 1953, and again the 'Bournemouth Belle'. The twins had been transferred to the Southern Region in March and April 1953, No. 10001 being the second to come across. It is likely this is also a Sunday working as the roster for the engine was this solitary turn from Nine Elms at the time. Later they worked on both Bournemouth and Exeter services.

Turning now to the SR design engines and this is No. 10203, the third engine based on the SR design and with an uprated 2,000hp power plant. It is seen brand new at Waterloo in April 1954 on a test train. The smart black livery works well with the red and cream although according to Colonel Rogers in his biography of Robin Riddles, this was not the favoured choice for coach liveries.

Embarrassment en-route to an exhibition at Willesden 25 May – 4 June. No. 10203 is depicted at Norwood supposedly on its way to Willesden but instead derailed; it is difficult to see exactly which bogie/set of wheels is on 'olde England'. The briefcase on top of the buffer was definitely not part of the design! But one aspect was, and that was the curved profile of the body sides to match that of the Bulleid coaching stock. Note with No.10203 there is no connecting door in the event of multiple unit working.

On dynamometer trials with the WR vehicle at Woking. This would have been taken on either 5 or 7 July 1955 on the 1.00pm Waterloo to Exeter, loads of 425 and 464 tons respectively. The analysis of the results showed that No. 10203 was 'a coach better' than her smaller engine sisters, Nos 10201/2, and would also have improved upon the capabilities of a Swindon 'King' if working out of Paddington. It was not however considered to be the theoretical equal of a 'Merchant Navy'.

No. 10203 in charge of the down 'Golden Arrow' at Petts Wood. Despite having all five main line diesel engines operating on the Southern at this time, one of the difficulties remained in rostering the engines for maximum usage whilst ensuring footplate crews retained sufficient familiarity. The latter was a particular problem as a set of men in the top link might only work with the engine once every six or eight weeks (dependent upon how many turns there were in the top link). This in turn could be reduced further if, when their time came, the engine was out of use or otherwise unavailable.

Slightly closer this time – same train of course. The consist appears to be eight Pullmans and a van for luggage at each end. Later years would see the number of Pullman vehicles decrease and replaced by ordinary stock.

A fortunate chance at Worting in 1954. SCT was in the cab of one of the diesels – we are not told which – when he saw another of these machines passing underneath the flyover en-route to Salisbury. No numbers were given.

The only view of a Class 33 (D65xx) in the collection. This is D6549 at the Burghclere end of the derailment that occurred between the latter station and Highclere on the DNS line in March 1963. The tank cars are being lifted and swung clear of the crane before being taken to Burghclere for examination. The engine would then return to site to collect further vehicles.

The Broad Clyst Shunter

Above and opposite top: It is difficult to know what to say and exactly how to describe No. 49S, the Engineer's Department shunter at Broad Clyst. Built locally at Exmouth Junction, from the images it appears to be made of an amalgam of parts; a coach bogie, at least one SECR axle box cover, possibly a further SECR component in the form of the coach birdcage – there was one at each end of the remainder of sheet and corrugated material. Inside was a petrol engine whilst the presence of the buffers and coupling hook would tend to indicate it might well have been used to move vehicles at some point although probably not the Meldon hoppers seen in the background. No. 49S had been built at Exmouth Junction in 1940 and lasted until 1959. Did it even travel under its own power to Broad Clyst in the first place and did it ever venture out on to the main line subsequently? Livery is probably best described as 'non standard'. *Images S. C. Nash/courtesy Stephenson Locomotive Society*

Bottom: L1 No. 31757 at Eastleigh with an unidentified Terrier beyond. Withdrawn (on paper at least) from Nine Elms in 1961, it lingered on until 1963 when it was finally cut up. Presumably also at Eastleigh as this is a rare view of the oil burning boiler house and the new diesel depot behind.

ENGINEERS
DEPT
S.R
49

31757

Rebuilt
The Letters and Comments Pages

As ever we remain grateful to all who have taken the time and trouble to add additional information or comment upon features in past issues.

We start with **Graham Buxton-Smither** on the topic of the **RIGHT TO STOP TRAINS AT STATIONS** apropos various features in **issues 51-53**.

"Thoroughly enjoyable (No. 53) and as with 52 and 51, read in a single sitting. As a former user of the service from Windsor & Eton Riverside to Waterloo, I was particularly interested in Peter Tatlow's contribution and found George Reeve's 'One Evening in May' a delightful piece of nostalgia. I see you kindly included my musings on driver tipping in your letters pages which brought to mind an altogether different response to me by a driver, this time in the 1990s, and brings me to the question...

"Does the Duke of Norfolk have any special rights concerning the services through Arundel Station? An odd question you may correctly surmise but it was the memory of a very surly driver that brought back a memory.

The late Duke of Norfolk, Miles Fitzalan Howard, was a chum who I sometimes dined at my old club, the Naval & Military, and on the last occasion we met before his death in 2002, I joined him for a convivial lunch at Arundel Castle. It was one of those happy days I used to enjoy when I was still working in London as I had another engagement that evening at the Chelsea Physic Garden for an opera picnic to raise funds for a children's medical charity. I confided to Lady Georgina, Miles' daughter in law, that I had to catch a specific train or I'd be in real trouble as I was to be in the company of Prince Edward and Lloyd Grossman and so should not arrive after the Royal guest. The luncheon became ever more convivial until it got to the point that Georgina, remembering my need for the train, exclaimed that it was due to depart the station in 3 minutes. Horrified, I ran for the Gate at which Miles had kindly arranged a taxi, shouting as I left my companions, 'Tell them to hold the train – I'm on my way...

Early days at Swanage. What is almost certainly an O2 leaving the terminus for Corfe and Wareham.

"The taxi sped down the hill, through the town, over the roundabout and into the station forecourt which fortunately was by the upline. The platform entrance was near the front of the train and I ran through seeing that there was still a train on the platform and the small First Class section was right opposite. As I reached the train, grabbing the door-handle, a very surly driver, hanging out of his window, looked at me and said something along the lines of: 'I suppose you're the **~!~~**! bloke that we've had to wait for?' and his face disappeared from view with those words ringing in my ears. Someone closed the door behind me and off we went. Thankfully, the return journey was otherwise uneventful and we arrived in London on time.

"I just took it for granted that Miles had told the train to wait but after more sober reflection, I now wonder if he had merely prevailed on the station staff to do him a kindness and let me on. Hence my question; I'm aware that some landowners have certain rights over services operating on their land and wondered if the Dukes of Norfolk have any such entitlements at Arundel Station?

"As you might imagine, I dined out for weeks on the story of the day that Network SouthEast (or whichever operator it was) held a train for me, knowing it would never happen again. But I enjoyed the acerbic comment of the driver which had me chuckling most of the way back to London and I sometimes recall it when I need to bring myself back to earth with a bump. I just wish I'd had the presence of mind to seek him out on arrival – I would happily have tipped him for waiting and the pleasant return journey but in these more modern, egalitarian times I suspect that had I done so, I might have missed my evening appointment, waking up eventually in A&E at Charing Cross Hospital..."

Ed – Graham raises a slightly wider question which has been missed by many who write the history of specific lines. We should not forget that at the time of railway construction, indeed we might even say up to the present day, vast swathes of land were in the hands of various estates which the railways had to cross to secure their route. Using (and I apologise for this) the GW as an example, the Duke of Beaufort required the line that passed across his estate at Badminton to be hidden as much as possible and with the vents for a two mile tunnel represented as castle turrets – they are still there today. He also had rights to stop trains at Badminton station. In addition to this, on my own favourite bit of GW line, the DNS, the Earl of Caernarvon insisted the station nearest his stately pile at Highclere Castle (of Downton Abbey fame, of course) be named 'Highclere'. It was, but subsequently gave rise to 75 years of confusion as Highclere station was in fact in Burghclere village, Burghclere station was in Sydmonton, and the proper name for Woodhay should have been Highclere – all very confusing. So were there places on the Southern, apart from Arundel, where 'rights' existed or perhaps still exist? Likewise stations named slightly incorrectly for the simple fact of political expediency? Comments would be welcome.

Now from **David Wigley** with **a question** and some interesting **follow ups.** We start with the question, **"**Can any 'Southern Way' reader provide the editor with a photograph of a train using the tramway that used to run from Feltham station to the R. A. S. C. depot south of the town? This is something which has been nagging me for some time. This line was connected to the down lay-by siding immediately on the country side of the Bedfont Lane level crossing. It traversed a quarter circle before proceeding down a public road, crossing Feltham High Street, continuing down another public road before entering the depot. It appears on the O. S. extract in Middleton Press 'Waterloo to Windsor' and also on the control diagram on page 86 of SW 53. Middleton Press state that the tramway had closed by 1958. I understand that it was worked by an '0395' from Feltham yard. When I was a youngster I was taken to the West end of Feltham High Street and shown where the trains ran down the road but I never saw a train use it. It is odd that there are no special instructions in the Sectional Appendix despite the street running and crossing a main road without physical protection."

Now to three items reference SW53, starting with the USA tanks on pages 29-30. David writes, "I doubt if any of these particular locomotives saw any WW2 service. I would suggest they are in exactly the same condition as when they left the builder's works ready for shipping. All the protection looks like a factory job. What is curious is the writing on five similar locomotives and every one lettered differently. You have already asked where? The track looks military and there appears to be an ex-LSWR restaurant car converted to an ambulance van beyond the smokebox of No. 1968."

"Page 68: the Ashford (Middlesex) up starting signal. This looks like a particularly awkward location for a signal, hence the unusual configuration. Signal sighting at Ashford was difficult as there are road overbridges at both ends of the station. In the foreground was the siding access to the goods yard and a further complication in the form of an authorised path from the yard to the platform as indicated by the kissing gate, notice and walkway. Presumably the platform ramp in this situation was deemed too narrow to accommodate a signal post. Hence the bracket signal. The customary 4-rail upright beefed up with diagonal bracing and the bought-in lattice bracket and doll."

"Page 73 'pigeons'. Racing pigeon keeping is not a common hobby in the South of England. However, from time to time lengthy trains of vans full of pigeon baskets plus a passenger coach for their handlers would arrive on the Southern for the birds' release, as at Winchester. In the late 1950s someone thought that the Southern Region should become involved in this traffic. Consequently twelve SR gangwayed bogie luggage vans which were otherwise being withdrawn were marked 'For Pigeon Traffic Only', attached to and marshalled into a train with a boat train matchboard 1st brake, and stabled at Tolworth. In reality the train only had a short life although individual pigeon baskets by passenger train were quite common. Esher station was also a well-used release destination being on an embankment and in open ground with the station staff recording the time of release on the basket."

The miniature railway that played its part defending the south's coastline. A genuine armoured train on the RH&D line.

An interesting snippet from **John Moon** on **Deepdene.** (John would also like to see more on the location if anyone can oblige – we have exhausted our own collection – Ed.) John comments that he is a former Southern Railway employee – just – having started work on 31 December 1947! He spent ten years on the railway, all with the CCE's department, firstly at Deepdene and later at Purley. John adds a comment that was perhaps fortunately not realised a few years before in WW2 which is that when Deepdene House was eventually demolished some years later, this was achieved with a wrecking ball on the end of a chain swung by a crane. The result though of hitting just one corner was that all four sides simply collapsed in on each other. Under such circumstances it was indeed fortunate the building was not bombed.

'Terrier' – v 'P' class on the Hayling Island branch. **Ross Shimmon** is still attempting to confirm the use of a 'P' class tank on the Hayling Island line and has perhaps moved a little closer with this comment, "I recently acquired 'Fratton Locomotive Depot, A brief history 1891 to 1967' by Michael G. Harvey, Kingfisher Productions (sadly, no date). On page 118 there is a photo of a 'P' at Fratton and with the caption stating that the 'P' had been loaned to Fratton from Brighton to replace an A1X that had gone to Eastleigh works in 1960." But can anyone still help further; *was* the 'P' used on the branch... ? (Again from Alastair Wilson, "I'm pretty sure that Fratton had no other use for its 'Terrier' than the Hayling branch, and I'm also pretty sure that I've read somewhere (but where?) that a 'P' was used on one occasion on the Hayling Branch".)

Finally for this issue, last but by no means least, some interesting and detailed information on the **workings of the main-line diesels** on the Southern from **Roger Whitehouse**.

"A caption on page 22 of SW44 raised questions about the Enginemen's Rosters when working the diesels, particularly on Exeter trains. The printed Engine Workings dated 14 June 1954, and until further notice, show that these followed exactly the same methods as when the trains were worked by steam.

"The wholesale revision of Engine Workings between Waterloo and the West of England from Monday 6 February 1950 eliminated many engine changes at Salisbury or Exeter, but, for Nine Elms and Exmouth Junction men, Salisbury remained a frontier town*, as shown in the accompanying Nine Elms Duties for the diesels."

* except for Nine Elms men working to and from Wilton on the *Devon Belle*.

To show what crews involved with the diesels were also doing, here are some details of other trains they worked in the London West & Southern Districts, ignoring weekend variations. Brackets () show the origin or destination of a train only partly worked by that crew.

Nine Elms Duty 1

N15	22	4.45am **P** Waterloo-Woking & 6.33am **P** Woking-Salisbury
MN	495	8.15am **P** Salisbury (6.50 Yeovil)-Waterloo

Nine Elms Duty 2

In the course of 24 hours, this engine was worked by 3 crews from Nine Elms and 5 from Bournemouth!

LN	425	10.33am **P** Bournemouth Ctl (9.20 Weymouth)-Waterloo
N15	263	1. 1pm **P** Bournemouth Ctl-Dorchester (Weymouth)
LN	425	6.30pm **P** Waterloo-Bournemouth Ctl (Weymouth)
LN	394	11. 15am **P** Bournemouth Ctl (11. 5 West)-Waterloo
N15	402	Bournemouth Ctl 4. 0pm shunt
		5.50pm **P** Ctl-West & 6.35pm **P** West-Ctl (Basingstoke)
H15	73	Southampton Ctl **F** (10.30pm Nine Elms)-Poole (Dorchester)
LN	426	9. 0pm **P** Waterloo-Southampton Dks

Nine Elms Duty 3

MN	497	2.15pm **P** Salisbury (12.30pm Exeter ACE)-Waterloo
MN	7	3. 0pm **P** Waterloo-Salisbury (Exeter)

Nine Elms Duty 5

S15	435	12.54pm **P** Salisbury-Waterloo
MN	495	6. 0pm **P** Waterloo-Salisbury (Exeter)

The Rosters west of Salisbury are available from a proof copy of the Western District Engine Workings. Trains worked by a diesel are in *italics*.

Salisbury Men

	1	*2.57.a.m. Salisbury (1.15 Waterloo)-Exeter Ctl*
MN	494	6.30am **P** Exeter Ctl-Salisbury (Waterloo)
	3	*12.28pm Salisbury-Exeter Ctl*
	1	*5.55pm Exeter Ctl-Salisbury*
MN	494	6.40pm **M** Salisbury (3.54 Clapham Jct)-Templecombe (Exeter Ctl)
	5	*9. 5pm Templecombe-Salisbury*

Exmouth Jct Men

MN	494	prepare for 6.30am **P** Exeter Ctl-Waterloo
	1	*7.30am Exeter Ctl-Salisbury*
	5	*10.56am Salisbury-Exeter Ctl*
MN	496	10.30am **P** Exeter Ctl-Salisbury (Waterloo)
	1	*2.45pm Salisbury-Exeter Ctl*
	3	*4.30pm Exeter Ctl-Salisbury*
MN	496	7. 6pm **P** Salisbury (5. 0pm Waterloo)-Exeter Ctl
	5	*6.48pm Exeter Ctl-Templecombe*
MN	494	**M** Templecombe (3.54 Clapham Jct)-Exeter Ctl

Abbreviations

F Freight

M Milk Train

P Passenger Train

Q Conditional

|| Light Engine

The commencing duty numbers for the depots involved are:

1 Nine Elms

251 Eastleigh

379 Bournemouth

425 Dorchester

429 Salisbury

494 Exmouth Junction

The class of engine is shown alongside each steam duty.

It is as well to remember that all working documents, such as the sources used here, record what was intended at the time of printing, not what actually happened."

Craftsman at Eastleigh. After introduction the cars worked on both the Southern and Eastern regions - seemingly John Elliott at Waterloo was glad to dispose of them as quickly as possible. Folklore also has it that the Carriage Works Manager at Eastleigh had the enviable task of touring Hampshire in his car looking for suitable names!

End of the line for a fine engine. No. 30936, formerly *Cranleigh,* stripped of name, coupling rods, valves and pistons and here awaiting its fate.
Paul Hocquard/The Transport Treasury

Finally we are as ever grateful to **Eric Youldon** for his own comments. These include some notes on the recent **S/W Special No 17** on the **'Oil Burning Engines'.**

P5 – To the LSWR should be added the SECR and SR.

P9 – Eric confirms the solidary D15 conversion, No. 463, was an excellent oil burner, "I had an excellent run behind it in April 1948 from Romsey to Salisbury on the 5.39pm Portsmouth & Southsea to Cardiff on what was a heavy train."

P29 – From a practical perspective now, Eric disagrees with the official line in that No. 740 was intended to visit all the loco depots where facilities were to be provided. This for the reason that in 1948 the 'King Arthur' class were in fact banned west of Exeter although in later years they were permitted as far as Meldon. No. 34036 did work a passenger service as an oil burner on 2 June 1949 when it was seen on the 10.30a. Exeter Central – Waterloo which it took as far as Salisbury. This is believed to have been the only time one of the two converted members of the 'West Country' class worked west of Salisbury as an oil burner.

P64 – Referring to Duty 364, the allocated engine should read 'T9 oil burner or L12'.

P70 – All five of the oil-burning members of the N15 type retained electric lighting for the rest of their lives.

P74 – First paragraph, for 'firebox' read 'smokebox'.

Exmouth Junction: Eric confirms the oil tank at this depot was indeed retained and used for water storage, a similar redundant tank was retained for the same purpose at Eastleigh.

Continuing on from the above and again with apologies for the running out of space in No. 55. We start with **Alan Holmewood** on the subject of **SW54 EMU headcodes** and the **wartime images** on **p93 and 94**. "Page 69. According to David Brown, headcode 58 was Victoria to Littlehampton via Redhill and Horsham. However, sometime between 1961 and 1971 Eastbourne to Ore was added to the list. I was originally unsure if the photo was taken at Eastbourne, but I'm now pretty sure that it was. So I suggest that the photo shows the Ore portion of an Ore to Victoria service and was taken after 1961 and before 1966, when the units were withdrawn.

"Page 93. The upper photo almost certainly dates from World War 1 as there are a number of women porters, who were employed by the railways to release men for the forces. Page 94. I would date this photo back to World War 2. Note the white railings and bollards in the foreground, the white running board on the car on the station approach and the white wing on the lorry behind it, and the white stripes on the station entrance canopy supports. London Bridge station was badly damaged by bombing, and I cannot work out from the picture if the top of the white station building has been partially removed after bomb damage or if it was built that way."

Railway Staff Halt at Wimbledon; No. 34089 *602 Squadron* will not be calling. *Paul Hocquard/The Transport Treasury*

Next from Mick Field. "Just a quick note on LBSCR D-TANK No.271 *Eridge* and its train at Hove. It's leaving to turn on the triangle, Brighton and Hove (via Preston Park). It is most likely a short working along the coast perhaps to West Worthing, or even shorter. It can't be much of a trip. The middle coach looks like a Craven, may be a 1St/2nd composite but that's only guess."

Bill Bishop is kindly able to provide some detail on S. R. Sisterson, referred to as being involved with the **Vortex blastpipe** trials. (**See SW54 pages 14-16.)** "The Sisterson on page 16 is George Robert Sisterson. He was a locomotive draughtsman under John Reid at Nine Elms, replacing him in 1902 when Reid retired as chief draughtsman to take up lighter duties in consequence of failing health, becoming the company's inspector of materials in his native Glasgow. The February 1903 edition of the 'South Western Gazette' noted the succession of Sisterson. He was an advocate of both compounding and superheating, neither of which were Dugald Drummond's favourite subjects. His resignation is noted in the September 1905 edition and it appears he became a consulting engineer. James A. Hunter was appointed chief draughtsman in 1906, arriving from the Metropolitan Railway.

"The 'Jubilee' on page 14 is also interesting. My first reaction was, what was a first series Jubilee doing with an Adams tender? Then I realised it was a dual braked locomotive, as these were paired with Adams 3,000 gallon tenders. Number 538 was initially paired with a Beattie 1,950 gallon, then maybe a Beyer, Peacock 2,500 gallon tender. Meanwhile eight of William George Beattie's '348' class were rebuilt by Adams and provided with new Adams tenders, but 348 itself did a swap with 538 in February 1893."

Len Wood also contributes along similar lines re **SW54.** "William Adams of the LSWR was an extremely gifted and brilliant engineer. His life story would make for an interesting publication*, It is a pity that he in 1895 had to retire; and what could have followed those four classes of 4-4-0s. ....?

"Drummond it seems, because of his fiery rhetoric, did himself no favours, apart from Eastleigh Works and the T9s. As regards the 4-6-0s, the less said the better, and I will add Cross Water Tubes and Steam Dryers under the same heading, basically an engineer who completely lost his way. How much too did this cost the LSWR? Indeed when passing through Exeter in the Bug, (to reach the far flung reaches of the LSWR beyond Cowley bridge), I wonder if he ever noticed the products of Churchward ?? Oh yes, for William Adams add the Vortex blast pipe." (* A fair assessment of the life of William Adams is given both in Bradley and also by Barry Curl in his book 'The LSWR at Nine Elms'.)

From **Peter Tatlow** reference the **Raynes Park derailment of 1967** and **p92, Purley**, both in **SW54.** "Pleased to see my article on the Raynes Park accident in print. Separately on page 92 you ask why the change to timber decking to the platform at Purley? The reason is because at that point the track passes on to the bridge over Godstone Road at 13m 33c and as this was a metal bridge, rather than masonry, purpose support to the platform was required. I recall that when I started work in the New Works Drawing Office at Waterloo in 1957, my colleague Denis Green, on the other side of the drawing bench, was designing the steelwork to support further platform extensions as part of the scheme to lengthen platforms prior to the introduction of 12-car trains at intermediate stations on the Brighton line."

This is a terrible quality image but it is staggeringly rare. It was lifted from a very obscure and old defunct newspaper. It shows the Freshwater, Yarmouth & Newport owned Drewry railcar in service entering Freshwater station, in itself a rare event as the vehicle was believed to have only been generally used if an engine failure occurred to either the Manning Wardle No. 1 or the Terrier No. 2, or if one of the boats at Yarmouth missed a regular train service. It could be hired too on the purchase of four first class or eight third class tickets, it is quite possible this photo was taken on one of those occasions. The view is the only full image of the original Stevens signal box (they were more like garden sheds!). It is also the only known clear view of the stop signal protecting entry to the station. Water tower, coaling platform and engine shed on the right. The railcar arrived soon after the FYN broke away from the stranglehold working agreement with the IWCR, exactly why it was purchased is unknown, but it was useful in an emergency, and of course only needed a driver. After the SR took over the FYN it may have been unsure what to do with it, they ended up numbering it in their carriage stock! Maycock & Silsbury, in their excellent book on the FYN, state it did see some use as an inspection vehicle from 1924 until it was scrapped in 1927.
Courtesy of Roger Simmonds

There will likely be nobody left who can recall the railcar in the previous view but this at least should be familiar. No. 34101 *Hartland* **disturbing the peace at Brockenhurst with a down working.** *K.R. Bloxham collection.*

Now from **Stuart Hicks** mainly on the topic of the **Raynes Park derailment, SW54**. "I can remember (vaguely, I was only 11 at the time, and brought up in nearby New Malden) the footbridge derailment at Raynes Park. As I recall, the footbridge was actually shut to passengers for some time (years) with interchange being required via the street, before it was repaired. The Wimbledon to West Croydon line was one on which I was taken on quite often whilst young (along with Waterloo for central London, and South Kensington via District line for the museums), including to the open day at Waddon power station, when a loco was in steam. Also p47, this is looking west at Vauxhall, so an up boat train." Stuart also asks, "Is Shirley Holms Halt (p78 in SW54) an April fool?" – *Stuart I can assure you not. I don't think we have ever included a deliberate April Fool in SW; just a few faux pas on occasions – Ed.*

Now from **Peter Broomhead** again on the topic of **shed codes** in **SW54. "**Having just enjoyed reading Issue 54, I am sure I am not the only one to get in touch to point out that 74E is not Three Bridges, but St. Leonards, and 30903 being stored there is perfectly logical as she was shedded there from 1948 to 1957, when the whole Schools allocation was transferred away.

"I have been an avid reader of 'The Southern Way' almost from the beginning (although bizarrely one of the first issues I purchased was at Gateshead Model Railway exhibition!), and have always meant to drop you a line to say how much I enjoy and look forward to each issue. I was brought up overlooking St. Leonards West Marina station, and can just about remember the Schools being shedded there. A little later, every evening, my father would take me and my younger brother over to the station to watch the local goods pass through, which in the early 60s was still steam hauled, usually by a standard 4MT 2-6-4 tank, or occasionally by an N or U class.

"Many thanks again for the goldmine that is 'The Southern Way' (although along with a lot of others I always bemoan the lack of Eastern Section articles – perhaps I could do one on St. Leonards West Marina at some stage!)." *Peter – you are most kind, thank you. I will admit I usually edit out gratuitous comments for this section although they are of course appreciated. Yours I left in as it raised a smile with your purchase at Gateshead. As regards something on St. Leonards, it would be most welcome. Similarly, there are literally hundreds of topics I would love to include but no one has volunteered and/or the material is simply not to hand – Ed.*

Turning away now from the ordinary editions and instead to **SW Special No 17** on the **Oil Burning Locos. Justin Edwards** has written and also sent some most interesting images. He writes, "I cannot add very much to what you already know but have a couple of comments regarding the LNWR tenders. I have two negatives I have purchased, but of these neither is of the quality of your picture. One is dated 9 August 1962 and shows the tanks in place. The other, undated, shows what I believe are probably the same tenders with no oil tanks. It was only after reading 'Southern Way' that I realised these were probably the Eastleigh tenders. Locomotive items dotted around marked Q, T9 and LN would seem to confirm the location. The tenders are the later design Bowen Cooke 3,000 gallon type. The pipe that runs up the back and appears to run into the original tender tank at the water filler has a vacuum hose type connection on it. Whether this was for drawing off, pumping liquid in or pressurising the tank to draw off liquid I have no idea.

"The tenders in your photograph at Eastleigh are not the same as the one in the Ashford photograph as the frames differ. The tender at Ashford appears to be an LNWR Whale 3,000 gallon. There is also a picture on Ian Nolan's Flickr site of a Whale tender at Lancing Works in 1963.

https://www.flickr.com/photos/31890193@N08/14190432036/in/photolist-nnvwg7-nBXF4j-nxRHpg-2jeoYCX-moAm5o-24Pxou2-2dLTZLa-oUYuR3-VFa57L-CNTBa6-E5rg3e-GgJb94-CNLSyY-LvBBVG-ccMHqy-6jSKDu

"Back in 2006 I came across a tank from an oil burning locomotive at a Somerset Quarry. The guide said it was bought ex-Army from the US Ordnance Dump at Masbury and had been made for French steam locos to be able to operate on oil sent over via PLUTO.

"Having looked at the 'Southern Way Special' it seems identical to an SR oil tank and I wonder if in fact it is actually from an SR oil burner (though possibly never used as such) and the guide was wrong. At the quarry it was used for oil storage though it has since gone from there."

Finally in this section from Alastair Wilson. In hindsight I feel I almost left myself wide open for comment consequent upon my Editorial in SW55. Alastair spotted this and has responded accordingly. "In your editorial for SW55 you asked: 'So how does one explain a railway interest to an individual whose likely perception is either an old man in a grubby anorak or someone called 'Kevin' – I blame my parents for that – taking numbers at a station?

Below and opposite: **The former tender oil tanks referred to by Justin Edwards.**

"In my case, it started with the steam locomotive – from an early age, I recognised its raw power – at the age of three (this is the 1930s), I used to scream blue murder if I wasn't taken in my pram down to Amersham station to watch the afternoon express from Manchester tear through at 3.15, usually headed by an engine with a name. As soon as I could read, I started to read the names, *Jutland, Marne, Somme,* and two unpronounceable ones*, Ypres* and *Aisne*. There was another one, which was lo-o-o-ong, *The Rt. Hon Viscount Cross, GCB, GCSI.* By this time, the war was on, and my father wasn't there to ask about the names, and I wouldn't ask my mother (women didn't Know About Railways – stand-by for brickbats – but I was also going on to comment that in your editorial list of those who 'share this harmless persuasion', you list no women).

"From noticing 'engines' ('locomotives' was a bit long to be able to spell with certainty), I started to notice that there were distinct types of trains, goods trains and passenger trains. I picked this up while playing in the 'Home Guard trenches', which lay in a field, just below the Met/GC line on its way to Great Missenden and points north. Goods trains 'clanked', but passenger trains didn't, and there were three kinds of passenger trains. There were two kinds which had always the same kind of engine on the front (I soon learned about the 'Whyte' notation), it was always an A5 4-6-2 tank engine: one always had six carriages (I never used the word coaches – a coach was a single-decker bus, a 'Green Line' which went all the way to London, and even out the other side); the other never had more than five carriages.

"By dint of going to London with my mother, I observed that the ones with six carriages went to Baker Street, and changed to having an electric engine at Rickmansworth, while the five coach trains all went to Marylebone, with a steam engine all the way. There were other trains, with varying numbers of carriages, hauled by an engine with a separate tender – these were 'express trains' which didn't stop at Amersham. One day, I saw a strange engine – it looked like one of the normal 4-6-2 tanks, but the wheels were the other way round, 2-6-4: it was shunting in the goods yard: and one day, one of this strange lot turned up on a passenger train. All of this meant questions, which started to be answered in some measure when I went to school, but which really started with the purchase of 'Trains Illustrated Annual 1947', still there on my shelves, closely followed by my first ABC – Southern Railway (we'd moved away to Sussex and I went to school in Surrey – electric country, not so exciting).

"In the meantime, I went to visit my grandparents from time to time at Williton in Somerset, where I found another railway with totally different-looking engines and different-coloured carriages, and I used to haunt the station, helped to push a van around the goods yard, and was even allowed up into the signal box to pull a lever (I think it was the level-crossing gate lock). I came to know some of the regular engines, an 0-6-0, No. 2212, and a 4-4-0 with a name, *Cormorant*, and an 0-6-0T (a pannier, but I didn't know that word at the tender age of 8), No. 1761 (I could remember that because it was just one away from the number of yards in a mile, which I'd just learned at school). More questions to patient railwaymen, always answered.

"I could go on but won't – but an interest in railways was a complete education in itself and has remained so. (Hence shelves and shelves of railway books – and that's another subject.)"

Book Reviews

LB&SCR Carriages Volume 4

Bogie Stock, 1906-1924

Ian White

Publisher: HMRS, Casebound

£35.00

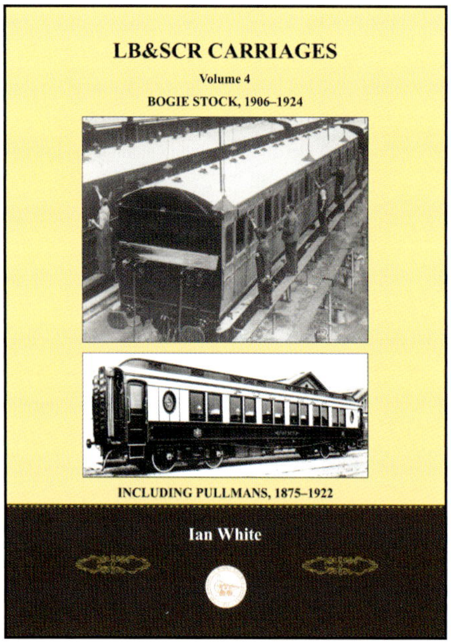

This is the final volume in the subject and this time with Ian White as sole author. Taking into account books produced by others on the SECR, LSWR and Southern, we now have a comprehensive account of most of the passenger vehicles that ever operated on SR lines.

As might be expected from an independent company, the LBSCR had a distinctive style all of its own, characterised not only by a distinctive roof profile but also in the use of innovations such as electric lighting; passed over nowadays without comment, but which would also not be totally standard on British Railways for a further four decades after the Grouping.

In eight chapters and eleven appendices, Ian's work covers and explains the various types of standard carriages, motor trains, Pullmans, proposals and saloons as well as the stock used on the elevated electric and the effect on rolling stock of WW1 including Ambulance Trains. Drawings, mostly to 4mm scale, are also included. The various appendices are similarly detailed and the book also contains Diagram and Running Numbers.

In a book of this type there can be a risk of it becoming repetitive, 'We turn now to the ...'. Ian has skilfully avoided this and whilst some readers may simply skip to their particular interest I would wholeheartedly recommend a more thorough read.

The old phrase 'a picture speaks a thousand words' is not forgotten here as illustrations abound in this work, there are over 200, and this does not include a large number of drawings. In addition where it is necessary to emphasise a point, the author/publisher have skilfully produced an enlargement of part of an image. Cruel it may be on the odd occasion but I have no issue with such inclusion.

Printed on art paper, for what it must be said is a highly specialist volume having very close to 300 sides (including prelims), this is very good value at the price.

Highly recommended to all Brighton, Southern and indeed rolling stock fans.

KJR

The Hythe & Sandgate Branch Line & Tramway

Peter A. Harding

Published by the Author and obtainable direct from him at:
'Mossgiel', Bagshot Road, Knaphill,
WOKING, Surrey GU21 2SG
ISBN 978 1 5272 8683 2
£4.50 +50p towards p&p

(Previously I have seen other examples of Peter's books on sale at exhibitions and at locations such as the Bluebell Railway shop.)

It is always a delight to see a new book from Peter Harding in his 'Branch Line' series and this latest one is no exception. There is a little phrase some people are wise to follow, simply put, 'If it ain't broke – don't fix it', and Peter has wisely followed this term by continuing the size, style and format of his latest title which fits in well with his previous books; hard to imagine there have been more than 20 already.

The Hythe & Sandgate branch opened from what would later be Sandling Junction station in 1874 and was extended of sorts with the opening of the first part of the Hythe & Sandgate Tramway in 1891. With high hopes for the railway, a double line was provided but traffic never materialised as predicted and the Southern Railway were left with no choice but to effect economies. The railway would close completely in 1951.

Peter's book, printed on quality art paper, describes the history of the line, how there was hope for an extension to Folkstone, a description of the route including station diagrams, and the motive power and rolling stock used.

He then turns to the Hythe & Sandgate Tramway including some delightful contemporary images of the horse drawn service in use.

This is the sort of book just about right for many of us. It tells enough to maintain the interest without going into what can often be drab political tales from long past history. If you are looking for an enjoyable evening's read than look no further.

The Leader Locomotive

Bulleid's Great Experiment

Kevin Robertson

Publisher: Crécy Publishing

£30.00

When the author (also our Editor, as I expect you know) first sent me the text of Leader, to be indexed, I remarked that it seemed to be a case of 'All you ever wanted to know about 'Leader' but were afraid to ask', and in a nutshell, that is what it is.

What it is *not*, is just a re-hash of a book of the same name which he first published 33 years ago, and subsequently updated. In his Introduction the author explains that his intention this time is to produce the story of 'Bulleid's Last Hurrah!' with more detail of "behind-the-scenes goings – on, the trials, and contemporary thoughts from someone who was there", and in this he has succeeded. In particular he now has access to the papers of John Click, who took part in some of the trials both in the UK, and on Bulleid's later version in Ireland.

Leader, an 0-6-6-0T, was Oliver Bulleid's conception of a do-anything, go-anywhere locomotive for the Southern Railway, (although all the Traffic Department wanted was a replacement for the M7 0-4-4T) and the building of five at Brighton Works was authorised by the Southern's General Manager, 11 September 1946. The design was packed full of innovations, one of them being the use of sleeve valves to control the passage of steam through the cylinders; another was the use of chains to couple the driving wheels in place of coupling-rods.

The first locomotive, No.36001, left the factory on 21 June 1949, and underwent trials from Brighton and Eastleigh (where it was known as the 'Great Grey Galloping Sausage'), until 20 November 1950, with mixed results. (The engine was rather like the nursery rhyme of the little girl with a little curl, right in the middle of her forehead – when she was good, she was very, very good, but when she was bad, she was horrid.) It was clear that a very great deal of re-design work was going to be needed if ever Leader was to succeed (for one thing, the weight was vastly over what was intended, or permissible), and with Bulleid now in Ireland, there was no one to stick up for the design, and it would definitely be a case of 'chucking good money after bad'. The final axe was wielded by Riddles as CME of British Railways, 20 November 1950. Work on the other four locomotives had ceased 26 November 1949, when 36002 and 36003 were nearing completion. (There is a chapter on 'Leader Mk.2', Bulleid's attempt at a similar locomotive for CIE, but burning turf (peat) as fuel. It was, on the whole, successful but, like Leader, too late – technology had moved on.).

The trial results are given in detail; and this reviewer found most valuable the Appendix entitled 'Leader – The Mechanics' by Les Warnett, who was a fitter at Brighton while Leader was being built, and was clearly an enthusiast for the engine. It gives a piece by piece description of the locomotive and all its ancillaries.

Bulleid was an innovator, but he must have known that trying out all these ideas at once in a new design was asking for trouble. While he was CME he could push forward the project, but nationalisation ended his authority.

The whole book is copiously illustrated, from the build at Brighton (despite a ban) through the trials (some images in colour) to eventual dismantling and despite all the detail is eminently readable. Recommended.

AW

The
Southern Way
The regular volume for the Southern devotee
MOST RECENT BACK ISSUES

The Southern Way is available from all good book sellers, or in case of difficulty, direct from the publisher. (Post free UK) Each regular issue contains at least 96 pages including colour content.

£11.95 each
£12.95 from Issue 7
£14.50 from Issue 21
£14.95 from Issue 35

Subscription for four-issues available
(Post free in the UK)
www.crecy.co.uk